Koon, Helene, 1925-

How Shakespeare won
  the West

$24.95

| DATE | | | |
|---|---|---|---|
| | | | |
| | | | |
| | | | |
| | | | |
| | | | |
| | | | |
| | | | |
| | | | |
| | | | |
| | | | |
| | | | |
| | | | |

How Shakespeare Won the West

# How Shakespeare Won the West

## Players and Performances in America's Gold Rush, 1849–1865

*by*

Helene Wickham Koon

McFarland & Company, Inc., Publishers

*Jefferson, North Carolina, and London*

British Library Cataloguing-in-Publication data available


Library of Congress Cataloguing-in-Publication Data

Koon, Helene, 1925–
*How Shakespeare won the West.*

   Includes bibliographical references.
   Includes index.
   1. Shakespeare, William, 1564–1616 — Stage history —
California.   2. Shakespeare, William, 1564–1616 — Stage
history — 1800–1950.   3. Theater — California — History —
19th century.   4. Actors — California — History — 19th
century.   5. Theaters — California — History — 19th
century.   6. California — Gold discoveries.
7. California — History — 1846–1850.   8. Frontier and
pioneer life — California.   9. Literature and history —
California.   I. Title.
PR3105.K66   1989      792'.0979409034      89-42727

ISBN 0-89950-432-9 (lib. bdg. : 50# acid-free natural
   and 70# enamel gloss papers) ∞

Manufactured in the United States of America

*McFarland & Company, Inc., Publishers*
   *Box 611, Jefferson, North Carolina 28640*

73 56 3239

To
Paul Zall
with gratitude for his three I's:
Ideas, Imagination, and Inspiration

# Table of Contents

# List of Plates

*Between pages 82 and 83*

*\* Photograph courtesy of the Huntington Library. The rest are courtesy of Nicholas Koon.*

# Acknowledgments

Special thanks for their care and assistance to Steven Green of the Searls Historical Library, Nevada City, and to the staff of the Huntington Art Gallery and Library, especially Susan Naulty.

Portraits of Catherine Sinclair, Matilda Heron, and Laura Keene are used by permission of the Huntington Library. Other photographs are by permission of Nicholas Koon.

How Shakespeare Won the West

# Introduction

A theatrical legend claims that the most popular playwright during the California Gold Rush was William Shakespeare. Improbable as it seems, the legend is true. Like some perverse Lochinvar, he came out of the East, gloriously ensconced in hundreds of theatrical trunks, as part of actors' standard equipment. Where actors went, there went Shakespeare.

Hundreds of actors and actresses played Shakespeare in the West. Many stayed only a short time, some remained for several years, a few settled permanently. All of them acted in more than one company and moved about frequently. To give some coherence, I have divided them into categories of certain shared characteristics. The division is arbitrary, but each chapter is roughly chronological.

This book, then, is the story of the actors, some famous, some quite unknown outside of the Western territories, who brought Shakespeare to California. It is not concerned with those who performed the many other kinds of plays, but only with those who, often in obscure camps and under the hardest conditions, made an Elizabethan playwright an integral part of the miners' lives.

It is not a general history of early theater in the West, already well covered by George MacMinn's *Theatre of the Golden Era,* nor does it center on the San Francisco theater, comprehensively portrayed in Edmond Gagey's *The San Francisco Stage* and the WPA histories. Although San Francisco was the heart of Western theater, it was only a small part of the total picture, for actors played all over the gold country. Almost every city and town from the ocean to Salt Lake City had at least one stage. Unhappily, few of their records escaped the many fires, but enough contemporary descriptions, reviews, and commentaries survive to give a fairly clear picture.

The Gold Rush era of 1849–1865 was a phenomenal time by any standard and from any point of view. The uprooting of thousands and the mad rush westward altered the face of the United States; in California, a shifting population of restless strangers created an intense and temporary way of life incomparably different from the rest of the country. The anomaly of Shakespeare's popularity under such circumstances reflects the strange, even exotic quality of that era.

# The Backdrop

Gold was discovered in May 1848, and before the year was out, the Western territories were almost depopulated in the rush to the mountains. It took somewhat longer for the news to reach the East, but the effect was the same. The population of California doubled, tripled, quadrupled, until it seemed as if the whole country was moving west. Those who could afford it went by ship, and steamship companies were mobbed for days before every sailing. Others went by land; by June, 1848, more than 12,000 wagons had crossed the Mississippi. However they came, whatever route they chose, the journey was an unforgettable ordeal.

Hard on their heels came the actors, and by 1851 the exodus was so great that New York managers were hurriedly signing the remaining players to long-term contracts in an effort to keep them there. Generally, they came by ship, bringing with them trunks filled with playscripts and keeping their skills sharp by performing on board. Most of the works were popular melodramas and farces but, among the playwrights, Shakespeare's name appears more often than any other.

When they arrived in California, they found an audience hungry for the theater of Shakespeare. The vision of rowdy, illiterate miners sitting in rapt silence through performances of

*Hamlet,* shouting lines to prompt forgetful actors, and paying great sums for the privilege of playing a favorite role is less fanciful than it might seem. Gold fever touched everyone from judges to farm hands, and Forty-Niners, and though often rowdy, were not illiterate. The average miner was between twenty and thirty years old, had at least a sixth grade education, and was familiar with Shakespeare, either because he had learned long passages from *McGuffey's Reader* or had seen a traveling theater company. He might even have played in an amateur production.

Theater was more than entertainment to uprooted Easterners, it was sustenance for the spirit. In spite of the occasional lucky finds, their lives were indescribably hard. They spent long days knee deep in water, digging, chopping, and washing the stubborn rock; at night, they slept on the ground or in canvas shelters; a diet lacking fresh foods brought scurvy and other illnesses; injuries were frequent and doctors rare. Above all, strangers in a hard land, they suffered from almost unbearable loneliness, and suicides were common. When they did find gold, they were eager to enjoy it, and they flocked into the towns. Drinking, gambling, and the few available women were the most common amusements, but plays, especially Shakespeare, offered a special kind of escape from the rigors of prospecting.

The first Shakespearean performances were by amateurs, but by 1849 professionals began to replace them, and the first real theater, the Eagle, was built in Sacramento. For all its historical importance, the Eagle was neither imposing nor long-lived. Attached to a saloon, it was a tiny structure of canvas and wood, thirty feet wide and ninety-five feet long. The roof was made of tin and sheet iron; rain produced a tattoo louder than actors' voices. The stage, built from packing boxes, was lit with kerosene lanterns, the auditorium floor was bare earth, and the seats merely rough board benches. It did, however, boast a "dress circle," a balcony reached from the outside via a ladder, so ladies would not have to go through the bar; to protect their modesty, the underside of the ladder was covered with canvas. The first performance was on October 18, 1849; on January 4, 1850, the theater was washed away by the flooding Sacramento River.

The company quickly moved downriver to San Francisco,

where they acted on a hastily constructed stage (also attached to a bar) and in an amphitheater housing a circus. Within a year, however, construction of more permanent quarters was under way, and San Francisco became the center of Western theatrical activity with anywhere between three and seven theaters, depending on how many were still standing after the last fire.

Because most actors came by ship, they landed first in San Francisco, where they generally received a hospitable welcome. Each time the city burned, larger and more elaborate theaters replaced the old, and by 1852, the major houses were as comfortable and well equipped as any in the country. The incessant fires discouraged no one, and building often began before the ashes were cold. Tom Maguire, the illiterate cab driver who became one of the biggest impresarios in the West, built three successive Jenny Lind Theaters.[1] The first (1850) burned down in six months, the second (1851) within two weeks, the third one (1852), a splendid palace with richly gilded decorations, was used as a theater only a few months before he sold it to San Francisco for their City Hall In 1853, he opened the Metropolitan, a pseudo–Renaissance structure iced with Greek and Norman Gothic details, "sumptuously furnished" and "brilliantly lit" with gas, its stage "fitted up with conveniences not to be met with in any similar establishment on this continent."[2] When it was destroyed by fire in 1857, he built his Opera House, the most elegant in his extensive chain of theaters stretching across California to Virginia City, Nevada.

The world outside the theater, however, was another matter. San Francisco's unpaved streets were choked with dust in the summer and so muddy in the winter that a full-sized piano could sink into the depths during a rainstorm. Lawlessness was rampant, food, housing, and laundry expensive, rats and fleas infested all buildings, public and private.

Sacramento, Marysville, and Stockton were even rougher, while the smaller towns were downright primitive. Not only were

---

1. *Although Jenny Lind herself never came to California, so many theaters were named after her that legends of her appearance on the West Coast still persist.*
2. Golden Era, *December 26, 1853. It was opened as the San Francisco Theater, but the name was soon changed, and it is generally known as the Metropolitan.*

the living quarters Spartan, but actors performed in hotels, saloons, houses — wherever a temporary stage could be set up. In the early years, especially, the rare structures that were not borrowed space but actually built as theaters were made of canvas and paper and lasted only until the next fire or flood. Few even had seats; patrons brought their own, staking out their places as fiercely as their gold claims.

Travel was slow and expensive. The 100-mile boat trip from San Francisco to Sacramento took ten hours and cost between eight and ten dollars, more than a day's pay for most. The sixty miles from Sacramento to Placerville was by land and took eight hours by fast stage, an uncomfortable and dangerous trip in springless wagons or stages. Highwaymen were common and the gold-bearing stagecoaches were fair game for them.

When players toured outside of established towns, they faced almost as many hardships as the miners. No roads led over the mountains and deserts, and trails were extremely vague. A single open wagon usually carried the actors, the trunks of costumes, and special stage properties. The slightest accident could bring serious consequences from the very real dangers of grizzly bears, wolves, sidewinders, and robbers. Weather was a constant problem; rain and snow made trails impassable, flash floods appeared without warning, high winds, laughingly called "Washoe zephyrs," blew men off their feet. And after facing such adversities, actors could not even be assured they would find a stage or a lodging house.

Yet the rewards were great. Actors, like miners, came for gold, and during the prosperous years it was plentiful. Salaries were in keeping with the expansive landscape. In San Francisco, Catherine Sinclair sometimes paid her stars $3,000 a week — in a day when Eastern theaters offered a tenth of that to their top attractions. That was, perhaps, excessively generous, but most stars could count on making about $6,000 for six successive performances. After two years, the Bakers went home with a clear $60,000, James Murdoch made $18,000 in eight months; in even less time, Joshua Proctor $15,000, Lola Montez $12,000, and Jean Davenport $5,000. Such income sounded astronomical, but expenses were also high, and, like the miners, actors spent almost as fast as they earned. James Stark made a fortune and lost it in silver mining, Junius Brutus Booth, Jr., in real estate, McKean Buchanan in a single poker game.

The real money was in touring. Miners, eager for any kind of entertainment, were appreciative audiences. In tiny settlements like Mokelumne Hill, Downieville, and Nevada City, centers of rich lodes, actors could earn as much in three days as in a week or more elsewhere, and Walter Leman, who toured almost constantly from 1856 to 1865, said that a traveling company averaged $300 a night throughout the gold fields. This was quite apart from the bags of gold dust and nuggets tossed on the stage at the end of a favorite's performance.

Mining camp hotels might be constructed of canvas and paper, their sleeping accommodations either infinitesimal cells or large empty second floors shared by all guests, but touring offered benefits besides gold. A bare hotel dining room furnished only with a central wooden table where the proprietor spent as much time shooing flies with a mop as he did waiting on people, provided wholesome and filling meals. Audiences were fanatically loyal to those they admired. They crowded the theaters, they applauded and cheered, they begged favorite actors to extend their visits, and when the time came to leave, they sometimes escorted a company to the next town.

If actors grew tired of roughing it, they could always return to San Francisco for a taste of luxury. Here the theaters were well provided with the necessities of production. Each had several "scenes," painted backdrops with matching side wings, showing a palace, a street, a landscape, and interiors "plain" and "fancy," which could be used for almost any play. Their property rooms were filled with wax fruit, imitation flowers, papier-mâché food, cotton-batting pies and cakes, plain and fancy furniture, with at least one throne or dais particularly useful in Shakespeare. A description in the *Alta California* gives an idea of the items required to create theatrical illusions in 1857:

> Here lies the sheet iron which supplied the thunder; there the peas which rattled against a sounding board, to indicate to the ears of the audience a furious rainstorm raging out of doors; in this side is a tube, like the spout of a watering pot, through which

powdered rosin was blown upon a flame, to make lightning; on
that side, the green cloth, sometimes stretched across the back of
the stage and shaken so that its undulations might suggest the idea
of the waters of a lake, sea, or river, to an imaginative public.

On tour, however, players travelled lightly and carried no
scenery. Bar seats doubled as royal thrones and their own trunks
as imperial treasure chests, kerosene footlights presented a constant fire hazard, while improvised entrances and exits through
windows made tragic dignity difficult to maintain. Typical of the
conditions was the stage at Sebastopol, "a town which could boast
of a hotel, store, blacksmith shop, corral and eight saloons," where
the show was given in the hotel's large garret:

> The boards and rafters of the garret were so scanty that the
> glorious climate of California could circulate in and out almost
> uninterruptedly.... The actors assisted by the landlord and the
> bartender had soon built a stage of rough boards, having on either
> side thereof horse blankets for wings; a blue and white flowered
> counterpane acted as stage carpet. When an immense American
> flag had been hung for a curtain their work of art was complete
> so far as the stage went. The space which had been left for the
> auditorium was filled with long boards poised on beer kegs. This
> was their arrangement for seating the audience. When the five
> candles stuck into beer bottles had been lighted for footlights, and
> the blind fiddler had screeched out the last notes of "The Arkansas
> Traveler," the curtain was pulled aside and the show began.[3]

The only way Shakespeare's rich atmosphere could be achieved
visually was through costumes. Shakespearean stars and leading
players usually had their own specially made. In the city, supporting actors could be outfitted from whatever stock the theater owned,
but they had to find their own shoes, boots, silk stockings, jewels,
swords, and feathers; touring companies furnished almost
nothing. Supernumeraries anywhere, hired for fifty cents a night,
were entirely responsible for their clothes.

Costumes had to be practical, colorful and, most of all,

3. The New York Dramatic Mirror, *January 3, 1908, p. 3.*

durable, while the exigencies of travel meant that they must also be kept to a minimum. The same boots, capes, uniforms and plumes served for any kind of play, modern or Elizabethan, and by 1854, some communities were already complaining that "Six dresses, two wigs and an iron sword constitute an ample wardrobe for a company of six to travel in the mountains."[4] Necessity also brought a good deal of license. For Macbeth, McKean Buchanan wore Western riding boots, a full-flowing cape, yellow gauntlets and a slouch hat. No one cared; historical accuracy was not important, even in New York, until the last quarter of the nineteenth century.

Casual as the physical aspects of production might be, the basic organization of companies was efficient and was based on a repertory system that dated back to the seventeenth century. True repertory, which required an established theater with a permanent company, was still possible only in cities like London and Paris. In such theaters, the same plays (between thirty and sixty) were given each season; new plays were occasionally added as less popular older ones were dropped, and the basic repertory changed very slowly. Actors, hired for an annual season, played the same roles from year to year, and many spent their entire careers in a single company.

The system was almost unknown in America, where the more practical stock company, an adaptation brought by English actors late in the eighteenth century, was the rule. The structure was essentially the same but considerably scaled down. The stock of plays was much smaller, the seasons shorter to accommodate the temporary nature of early American stages and the many touring companies. In the cities, some theaters became more or less permanent, but neither the repertories nor the companies were as large as in the old country, and they depended heavily on visiting stars to enrich their offerings. Their personnel varied; on the average, actors stayed at a single theater no more than three to five years. Even less stable were the touring companies that moved like gypsies across the states, often traveling on foot, stopping in small communities only long enough to present their small stock of four

4. Golden Era, *March 11, 1854.*

or five plays, regrouping and recasting frequently as actors came and went. Whether permanent or touring, however, the structure of companies was common to East and West alike.

The typical company had only eight to ten people. The star, the leading man, or the leading woman was the manager, a position that required a good deal of experience. Actor-managers, sometimes called "stage managers," were responsible for choosing the plays, hiring the cast, overseeing rehearsals (there was no such thing as a director), sets, costumes, advertising, and the box office. Touring managers also chose the route and made arrangements with the various theater owners. The rest of the company was made up of assorted types: juveniles and ingenues, character men and women, a comic or two, and at least one "utility player," who served wherever needed.

All actors were expected to play a wide range of parts in a variety of plays. The bulk of the repertory was contemporary, but every company included some Shakespeare, and any experienced actor could play his works at short notice. This was especially important in the West, where playbooks were scarce and productions were often determined by the repertories of the available actors.[5] The number of characters in a Shakespeare play was more than most companies could supply, but they managed by cutting and adapting the scripts, by doubling or even tripling roles, and, in extreme cases, by hiring amateurs to fill out the cast.

Although actors were familiar with the standard Shakespeare plays, the frequent moves from one company to another often required them to memorize new roles quickly, and they learned tricks to cover lapses of memory, incorporating them into whatever part they played. Surefire bits of comedy (the *lazzi* of the commedia dell'arte, the *schtick* of modern comics) or topical jokes covered a multitude of sins. Some went too far, and eventually critics complained bitterly about,

> the disagreeable habit which actors have of interpolating words, sentences, and even sentiments, for which they can find no warrant in their parts as set down for them by the author. . . . [Some]

5. *This was a particular problem in the early years. John McCabe said the Eagle had so few books that a copy of* Box and Cox *cost one ounce of gold dust.*

have been so long indulged in as to have acquired a kind of prescriptive right to keep their places.[6]

Such improvisation was more likely to happen in road companies than in the cities where productions were more finished. It is true that touring performances were apt to lack polish, but they were probably no worse than their counterparts in the frontier playhouses of Kentucky, Illinois, or Missouri. Transplanted Easterners, however, were quick to point out the flaws, and a Nevada City performance of *Richard III* was loftily criticized by a visiting English journalist:

> Next door [to his hotel] was a large thin wooden building, in which a theatrical company was performing. They were playing Richard, and I could hear every word as distinctly as if I had been in the stage-box. I could even fancy I saw King Dick rolling his eyes about like a man in a fit, when he shouted for "A horse! A horse!" The fight between Richard and Richmond was a very tame affair; they hit hard while they were at it, but it was soon over. It was one-two, one-two, a thrust, and down went Dick. I heard him fall, and could hear him afterwards gasping for breath and scuffling about on the stage in his dying agonies.[7]

Such a performance could easily have taken place in any frontier theater, East or West. The only difference was in the audience; in the West, it was almost exclusively made up of young males who liked powerful, energetic acting. Yet if their taste leaned toward the forceful, it was also sound, and they measured actors by the high standards of Junius Brutus Booth, Laura Keene, the Chapman family, and Julia Dean Hayne. Shakespeare was taken seriously, and those who did not measure up were pelted with vegetables and sometimes driven from town.

The miners may have felt a special kinship with Shakespeare's larger-than-life characters, perceiving them as living epic lives like themselves. Their own quest for gold, their hardships, the very scenery around them was larger than the world they had known

6. Golden Era, *February 22, 1857.*
7. *J.D. Borthwick,* The Gold Hunters *(New York: Doubleday, 1917),* 183–84.

back East, and they could see their own feelings mirrored in the powerful emotions. The violent confrontations of an Othello or a Macbeth were paralleled every week on the streets of Poker Flat and Hangtown. Not even the language troubled them. The ringing Elizabethan eloquence was not alien to a generation reared on the cadences of the King James Bible.

More than half of the canon was given in the West, although the frequency of performance varied widely and depended on the manager's choice.[8] Some were given several times each year, others only once or twice during the entire Gold Rush; *Antony and Cleopatra* and *The Tempest* were played only in burlesque versions. Surprisingly, more tragedies than comedies were played, possibly because stars made their reputations in tragedy, possibly because comic plays were more likely to be contemporary.

The plays were seen in heavily revised versions. In the theater, fidelity to the scholarly text has always been considered secondary to dramatic effectiveness, and actors have never felt inhibited from adapting Shakespeare's text to fit the needs of the company or the taste of the audience. Since the Restoration, his plays had been cut, with scenes transposed, interpolations added, and even the endings changed. "Acting versions" in which the alterations were indicated by quotation marks, were published and commonly used in the theater. English actors favored the Inchbald or Lacy texts "from the Theatre Royal, Drury Lane," while Americans tended to rely on the Cumberland series published in Philadelphia. These versions became so traditional that the painfully researched library text was almost forgotten.

The most popular Shakespeare play was Colley Cibber's version of *Richard III*. Cibber had cut a number of characters, lifted scenes from *Henry IV, Part 2, Henry V, Henry VI,* and *Richard II,* focusing the action on Richard to make a fast-paced melodrama. Audiences knew and loved it so well that every star, every would-be star, even child prodigies gave it at least once or twice each season.

---

8. *Plays that were not put on:* All's Well That Ends Well, Henry IV, Part 2, Henry V, Henry VI, Parts 1, 2, 3, Love's Labours Lost, Measure for Measure, Pericles, Richard II, Timon of Athens, Titus Andronicus, Troilus and Cressida, *and* Two Gentlemen of Verona. *Those performed are cited in the text.*

The original version did not return to the stage until almost the end of the nineteenth century.

*Hamlet,* of course, was also a perennial favorite and suffered almost as many changes. In an effort to make the prince as noble as possible, "O, what a rogue and peasant slave am I," Hamlet's cruelty to the Queen, and his teasing of Ophelia were omitted as showing an undesirable baseness of character. Hamlet was young, romantic, athletic, and the fencing scene was always a high point of excitement. The First Gravedigger, played by the company's low comedian, usually rewrote his part to include topical jokes, while minor characters like Osric, Rosencrantz and Guildenstern, and Fortinbras were regularly cut, and the play ended with Hamlet's death.

As a melodrama, *Macbeth* was played at least as often as *Hamlet* and for practical reasons was probably more popular among the touring companies. The cast is relatively small, and several parts could be combined: Seyton with several of the servants, Macduff with Ross, Angus, and Lennox. The battle scenes were always spectacular, and in more elaborate productions, it was embellished with music, most notably "Singing Witches."

The earliest tragedy played in California was *Othello,* an amateur performance at Sonoma in 1849. A year later, the first professional production took turns with the circus at Rowe's Olympic Amphitheater in San Francisco. Many stars liked to alternate playing Othello and Iago, with the latter a slight favorite. The emphasis was on the evils of jealousy; no one, even as the Civil War approached, seems to have been concerned with the black/white question.

Except for James Stark, actors used Nahum Tate's seventeenth-century adaptation of *King Lear.* Tate added a moral by inventng a "pure" love between Cordelia and Edgar and setting it against the illicit triangle of Goneril–Edmund–Regan. He also gave the play a fairy-tale conclusion; Lear does not die, and the goodness of Cordelia and Edgar is rewarded with the English throne. The changes appealed to moralists who felt Shakespeare's ending was unjust.

*Romeo and Juliet* was also changed, although the ending remained tragic. Here too the emphasis was on the purity of the young lovers, aged to a more socially acceptable eighteen. All mention of Romeo's earlier love, Rosaline, was omitted, he was not allowed to kiss Juliet at their first meeting, and Juliet's grief over his banishment did not include the unfilial suggestion that she would rather have lost her parents. The play ended with the deaths of the lovers, the reconciliation of the two families replaced by a showy funeral procession.

One might expect the patriotic fervor of the time would make *Julius Caesar* a stock play, but in spite of its murders, battles, and great declamatory speeches, it was rarely acted. The reasons are not entirely clear. Possibly the lack of a clear-cut starring role made it less attractive to actors, possibly the audience had little classical background — *Antony and Cleopatra, Titus Andronicus,* and *Timon of Athens* were not given either — but a more likely reason is the costumes. Although considerable freedom was allowed, there were limits, and all these plays require crowds of toga'd figures. In the other plays, costumes were interchangeable, but few actors could afford to carry about costumes limited to a single work, especially costumes which, to the American mind, were somewhat ridiculous. The only other Roman play performed was *Coriolanus,* and that only once or twice.

The most popular comedy was David Garrick's version of *The Taming of the Shrew,* renamed *Katharine and Petruchio,* with the Christopher Sly story omitted and the action concentrated on the two leading characters. Played like a farce, it offered opportunities for a great deal of slapstick, and it was in almost every repertory.

Almost as great a favorite was *The Merchant of Venice.* The play was adapted to star Shylock as an arch villain, with Portia (played by the ingenue) clearly a subordinate role. The casket scene was usually omitted, and Shylock's defeat in the end was regarded as a thoroughly moral lesson for all.

Other comedies were performed only rarely. *Much Ado about Nothing* was seen more often in the city than in the small towns and camps, as were *As You Like It* or *Twelfth Night,* despite the allure of actresses in tights. Only a well-equipped theater could manage Laura Keene's lavish *Midsummer Night's Dream,* while *Comedy of Errors* requires twins, or at least players who resembled each other. Alexina Baker and her sister, Oceana, played it, so did the Denin sisters; *The Two Dromios,* a version stressing the low comedy, featured Edwin Booth, but such productions were rare. An 1860 performance of *The Merry Wives of Windsor* starred the greatest Falstaff of the age, James K. Hackett, and a single production of *The Winter's Tale* was highly praised but never became part of the repertory. *Cymbeline* was not seen until Adelaide Neilson brought it out in 1864. It came and went with her.

Shakespearean history plays had little to say to Westerners unfamiliar with England's past. *Henry VIII, Henry IV, Part 1,* and *King John* were performed in San Francisco, but they needed such lavish settings to make them palatable that they were not part of touring repertories.

All plays, even the most profound tragedies, were followed by afterpieces, usually farcical one-acts, an antique theatrical tradition that stretched back to the seventeenth century. These not only filled out the evening's entertainment and provided a relief from the somber emotions of a Lear or Hamlet, but gave actors an opportunity to display their versatility. Tragic actors need not feel frustrated in their desire to make people laugh when they could clown their way through a comic afterpiece. The custom lasted until World War 1.

Shakespeare's popularity reached its height in the seven years between 1849 and 1856, when the gold madness flourished and hard earned nuggets were freely spent. In the crude amateur productions of the early years as well as in later starlit extravaganzas, he was in the truest sense, popular culture, and the performances of his plays reflected this age of romance, of unreal dreams and very real fortunes, of wild-eyed dreamers and hard-headed realists, all larger than life.

The reflection altered as the times changed, for, more than any other art, the theater is affected by current events. Weather, natural disasters, and the local economy directly affected the box office, determining the success of productions and the survival of companies. Extremes of heat and cold influenced theater attendance; rain, particularly in the early years, made the streets so muddy that even short-distance travel was very nearly impossible, and some enterprising managers, eager for women to attend, offered carriage service to and from the theater. Depressions and droughts had a devastating effect on the box office; when gold was readily available, the theater enjoyed a prosperity that disappeared when hard times came. Even politics affected performances; in the middle of *The Merchant of Venice,* a shot from Telegraph Hill told San Franciscans that returns from the 1856 presidential election had arrived. The entire audience rose and left the theater.

In the overall picture, certain patterns can be seen. From 1849 to 1851, when performances depended on who and what were available, productions were fairly crude and amateurish. The years between 1852 and 1856 saw the arrival of stars and fine actors, the building of theaters, and the development of a distinctive audience taste. Shakespearean productions did not end abruptly in 1856, but the frequency and kind began to alter. During the next decade and a half, the Civil War, the development of the cross-country railroad, and the regular appearance of nationally known stars with their own companies changed the emphasis once and for all. Shakespeare the popular culture figure became Shakespeare the art form.

At the same time, his audience was also changing. When gold became less accessible, expensive equipment was necessary to dig it out of the earth, and only large companies could afford the investment. The great river of immigrants slowed to a trickle. Many prospectors returned home; of those who stayed, some went to work for the mining companies, others took up former trades or professions, while the unreconstructed continued their search in more distant fields. Men married or sent for their wives, churches and schools replaced the rows of saloons, and the camps, particularly where the mining industry flourished, became solid communities much like those in the East. Echoes of the earlier exhilaration were occasionally roused by new strikes, and a miniature rush took place when silver was discovered in Virginia City, Nevada, but in most places, actors were no longer rewarded with bags of golden nuggets. Miners had families to support.

As the opportunity for quick fortunes diminished, fewer actors made the trip West, and those who came tended to rely on the attraction of surefire melodramas and contemporary comedies. Still, theater remained a favorite entertainment, and if Shakespeare's army changed its allegiance, it did not leave the field completely. He was still in the repertory, still a favorite of stars and would-be stars, and San Francisco marked his tricentennial on April 23, 1864, with grand productions of *Macbeth* and *Midsummer Night's Dream*. It was a fitting conclusion to an extraordinary era.

# Soldiers and Amateurs

## *The Military*

Shakespeare first appeared in California by grace of the United States Army some time before the Gold Rush began. He would, no doubt, have arrived sooner or later as the country expanded westward, but his advent was hastened by the Mexican War (1846–1848) which brought an influx of soldiers. Among these were the Seventh New York Volunteers, who enlisted with the understanding that after their term of service was finished, they would remain in California for at least three years and bolster the United States' claim to the territory.

Under the command of the redoubtable Colonel Jonathan Drake Stevenson, a politician who gained his command by virtue of his connections in Washington and his capacity to raise a regiment, they left New York on August 26, 1846, on the six-month journey arond Cape Horn. For many, it was their first time away from home, and they suffered from seasickness, overcrowded quarters, and bad food. Essentially civilians, they met military discipline with threats of mutiny until Stevenson threatened to blow up the ship. It was something of a blessing, then, when William H. Maxwell, a stage-struck young New Yorker, opened his trunkful of playscripts somewhere off the coast of Argentina.

Amateur theatricals were a favorite American pastime in the

nineteenth century. Requiring little except enthusiasm and such costumes or props as could be easily found, plays were considered harmless amusement and were commonly performed for family or community entertainment. The fare was mostly tableaux, farces, or melodramas, although now and then an ambitious group would choose Shakespeare, more because his texts were easily available in print than because of artistic preference.

Maxwell's trunkful of plays, then, was enthusiastically welcomed, and the threat of mutiny evaporated as the Volunteers rehearsed and performed their way to San Francisco. It was not always easy. Sometimes the sea was so rough they had to use ropes to keep from falling, scenery was minimal, properties were whatever could be found, and women's costumes were borrowed from the few wives on board. Wives, of course, were not included in the all-male casts.

When they landed in March, 1847, General Kearney took command of the regiment. Well aware that the Volunteers were not seasoned warriors, Kearney wisely assigned them to guard duty, a dull contrast to the adventurous life they expected. Most were sent to Monterey and Santa Barbara, a few remained at the San Francisco Presidio. Of these, Company C was soon ordered to Sonoma where they relieved their boredom by putting on plays as they had done on shipboard. They had considerable assistance from Sonoma's founder, Don Mariano Guadalupe Vallejo. Friendly to the Americans, he loaned them a building on his estate, thus establishing the first regular theater in California.

Company C performed no Shakespeare, however, and the honor of introducing him to California belongs to the Santa Barbara contingent, among whom was Maxwell and his trunk of plays. These troops spent the summer of 1847 remodeling a large adobe house into a theater and performing the most popular Shakespeare play of the nineteenth century, *Richard III*. With two blankets for a curtain, lambskin wigs, and an orchestra of two guitars, a violin, and a drum, the production showed considerable enterprise and ingenuity.

The company continued to act after they were transferred to Los Angeles in the spring of 1848. Here, their accommodations were somewhat more elaborate, for Don Antonio Coronel, even more generous than Vallejo, gave lavishly of his own money to build a theater of 300 seats. The audience area was unroofed, but the stage was covered with ample room for a drop curtain and a little scenery. The only condition was that they share the quarters with a troupe of Spanish actors.

Their season was brief, cut short by two events that profoundly affected the whole country: the discovery of gold at Sutter's Mill in January and the Treaty of Guadalupe Hidalgo that ended the war with Mexico in May. Between the two events, gold fever had triggered a flood of desertions that might have proved a serious problem for the army had the volunteers not been mustered out almost immediately. Most of them kept their promise to stay in California. They went straight to the gold fields.

The military theaters in Sonoma and Los Angeles closed, Sonoma permanently, Los Angeles only until the arrival of Major Graham and his dragoons, one company of which boasted at least two former professional actors, John ("Jack") Harris and C.E. ("Ned") Bingham. Although still in their mid-twenties, both had been on the stage for several years.

Harris was the more experienced, having played Mercutio in *Romeo and Juliet* and the title roles in *Mazeppa* and *Richard III*. A Philadelphian, he had made his debut at the Walnut Street Theater in 1829, had acted in Boston, New York, and a number of touring companies. For a time, he was the juvenile lead in a Mrs. Pritchard's troupe, which played frontier towns in Missouri, Louisiana, and Texas.

Bingham was a St. Louis man, but he had acted in New York while still in his teens and, in 1843, in Noah Ludlow's company at the St. Charles Theater, New Orleans. Like Harris, he had toured, and he too was in Mrs. Pritchard's troupe, where he probably met Harris. The two young actors became fast friends and enlisted in the same company during the Mexican War.

They saw active service with Zachary Taylor in Mexico, but they were actors at heart, and they soon organized a theatrical group among their comrades. Like Stevenson's Volunteers, the dragoons harbored many amateur thespians, and whenever the army paused, they performed. In Monterey, they gutted three houses, laid in a stage and a tier of boxes, and played a sizable repertory that included *Hamlet*. Unlike the Volunteers, however, they had two professionals who not only supervised rehearsals but collected a good supply of scenery and costumes. They also had the advantage of a competent actress for leading women's roles — Bingham's wife traveled with him. When the company was ordered to California, scenery, costumes, and Mrs. Bingham went along.

The dragoons arrived in Los Angeles in January, 1849. At once they set prisoners to work refurbishing the theater, cutting a trapdoor in the stage, and hanging the scenery they had brought. In a month, they were ready to give the first West Coast *Hamlet,* with Harris in the title role. It was a bare taste of the play, consisting only of acts one and five, but a good choice for a group of soldiers with only seven actors among them. One man divided his energies between the Ghost (with a sensational exit through the trapdoor) and Laertes; another had the triple responsibility for Polonius in the first part, the Grave Digger in the fifth, and the foppish Osric at the end. Mrs. Bingham played Ophelia, and a Mrs. Wentzel, newly added to the company, the Queen.

*Hamlet* was their swan song. By the time it was given, the war had been over for a year, the Gold Rush was in full force, and on May 16, 1849, the dragoons were mustered out. Harris and the Binghams went north to enter the burgeoning professional theater, Harris to Sacramento, the Binghams to San Francisco.

The last of the military actors performed in Monterey. In January, 1849, a handful of Company C veterans gathered together and, with contributions from their old friend Vallejo, ex-Governor Boggs, and Colonel Victor Prudhon, they fitted up a tiny theater formerly used by Spanish players. Exactly where this stood is not known, but the most persistent claim has been for the sailors' headquarters established by Jack Swan in 1846, a building still used for plays.

Here, in the spring, they gave the California premiere of *Othello,* a condensed version with an all-male cast. Colonel Prudhon played the title role, and at least four other former volunteers took part: C.V.R. Lee and his brother, who had been part of the group since the early shipboard performances, A.J. Cox, later editor of the Sonoma newspaper, and John Rowe, a specialist in women's roles. It was a kind of last fling before getting on with lives that had no room for theatricals. Of the four, only Rowe continued on the stage. Four years later, he was a professional dancer in Hawaii, still occasionally playing female roles.

Veterans from Los Angeles replaced the Company C men in the Monterey theater, and the following year they also chose Shakespeare for a farewell appearance. With scenery and costumes brought from the south, they offered *The Story of the Gadshill Robbery,* excerpted from *Henry V* in February, 1850. It was probably a burlesque played for the fun of it, and they listed themselves as "Forrest," "Booth," "Macready," "Kean," "Kemble," and other famous actors of the day. This gala occasion marked the last of the military productions.

Shakespeare had come to California almost by accident. He was hacked to bits, paraphrased and parodied in performances that were neither memorable nor great. The military productions did not mark a giant step in theater. They did, however, introduce him to a new and interested audience and provide a springboard for the future.

## The Amateurs

The end of the military theater did not mark the end of amateurs. Like the soldiers, prospectors were used to theatricals, and from the earliest years such unlikely places as Git-up-and-Git, Hell's Delight, Rat Trap Slide, Centipede Hollow, and Skunk Gulch were so hungry for any kind of performance that they went to great lengths to provide a space that, with the judicious arrangement of materials at hand, could be used as a stage. Later on, the newly established small towns provided local residents with more or less traditional theaters.

In makeshift or permanent accommodations, those who could sing, dance, or recite provided entertainment. Plays, however, required more elaborate preparations, and since few prospectors had the time or taste for long rehearsals, amateur drama was less common than in the East. Furthermore, while nonprofessionals were unlikely to know the lines of modern plays, they were familiar enough with Shakespeare to approximate the speeches and minimize rehearsal time. Therefore, if amateurs wanted to act, the most likely choice was one of his works.

Inevitably, some of them became fatally stage-struck and longed for stardom. The lucky ones found a willing company of professionals who could support them and make them look good. In San Francisco, a "celebrated Eastern amateur," Mr. Carleton, played *Othello* with Nesbit McCron's company on February 4, 1850. He reaped no laurels from the performance but neither was he censured, perhaps because any drama was welcomed at that time. McCron replaced him in the role a month later, and Carleton's name is never mentioned again. Few amateurs were so fortunate.

Miners were uninhibited in their response to a performance; their criticism ranged from the verbally acerbic to the physically embarrassing, as one ambitious hopeful discovered when, after much pleading, he was allowed to play the tent scene in the amateur's favorite role, Richard III. The event took place in Mokelumne Hill, where a group of would-be thespians had constructed their own theater. It was somewhat better appointed than most frontier houses and even had an ingenious arrangement for footlights: a board holding a row of candles that could be raised and lowered through a slot in the front of the stage. The night of *Richard* is best told in the words of J.J. Ayers, who was present:

> The house was crowded. It was a dark stage. Richard was writhing on his couch. The ghosts of King Henry, Clarence, Rivers and Buckingham had worked him in his sleep up to concert pitch. With a frantic bound he leaped from his couch and rushed to the front of the stage with his sword beating a tattoo on the boards . . . falling on his knee, he cried out to the people in front to bind up his wounds and give him another horse. As he made this appeal in tremulous tones a musical burro which one of the boys had mischievously fastened under the stage answered his prayer in corrugated notes that made the rafters shake. A great roar went up from the audience. The prompter, who could not see the front of the stage, thought the time had come to raise the footlights, and as the unabashed tragedian pathetically appealed to heaven and cried, "Have mercy, Jesu," one of the lighted

candles bobbed up against his nose and brought the scene to an abrupt end.[1]

The infuriated actor left the stage and never tried Shakespeare again.

The nadir of the Richards was reached by Hugh McDermott, who posed as a "master tragedian" but was undoubtedly an amateur in the worst sense of the word. By the time he played Sacramento in December, 1856, his reputation had preceded him. The evening paper, the *Union,* reported that while only a few carrots were thrown in the first act,

> The stabbing of King Henry was too much for the audience, more particularly the home thrust, *a postieriori,* after Henry had fallen. Cabbages, carrots, pumpkins, potatoes, a wreath of vegetables, a sack of flour and one of soot, a dead goose, with other articles, simultaneously made their appearance upon the stage.

The dead King Henry fled, roused from death by a well-aimed potato, and Richard soon followed, "his head enveloped in a halo of vegetable glory." He returned for the next act, but another deluge of edibles, this time accompanied by Chinese firecrackers, drove him permanently from the field.

Such a demonstration might discourage some, but McDermott was nothing if not determined. On Christmas Eve, he repeated his performance in Nevada City, and the event was reported by Harry Wells in his *History of Nevada County:*

> The entrance of Richard, in the form of the awkward and ungainly tragedian, was received with a burst of laughter, and as he proceeded with his lines, his voice, now swelling into the whoop of a Comanche, now sinking into a broken wail of unutterable despair, was answered with whoops and wails of feline love-songs from the convulsed audience.

Again McDermott stubbornly proceeded, but as he spoke the lines, "and all the clouds that lowered on our house in the deep bosom of the ocean buried..." he was interred under a fusillade

1. *Colonel James J. Ayers,* Gold and Sunshine *(Boston: Gorham, 1922), pp. 103–106.*

of vegetables. Harder objects soon followed, but McDermott dog-
gedly continued. The most humiliating moment, however, came
when he bared his breast and offered to let Lady Anne plunge a
sword in his heart. With one voice, the entire audience roared,
"Kill him! God damn him! Kill him!"[2]

McDermott was not the only casualty. At the end of the
performance, the infuriated audience rode his agent out of town
on a rail. No one sympathized with him, and the papers observed
tartly, "If it be true as stated, that he is the mountebank, while
McDermott is the tool and victim, should he next be treated to a
coat of tar and feathers he will get no more than he deserves."[3]
Apparently McDermott took the hint, for no more attempts are
recorded, but his name was remembered. A year later, the *Golden
Era* condemned an actor by stating flatly that his "comedy is
inferior to McDermott's."

The other favorite Shakespearean hero was, as might be expected, Hamlet, usually played as a dashing romantic hero with
emphasis on the fencing scenes. In spite of its allure, the role is exceedingly difficult to sustain and, lacking the concentrated evil of
Richard, apparently had less appeal for melodrama-minded
amateurs. At any rate, not as many attempted it. As a standard
in every professional repertory, however, the play was familiar to
all, and filling the cast with supporting amateurs was never a
problem.

One such performance took place in 1854 after a series of
events almost as dramatic as the play itself. That spring, Ayers was
co-managing the theater in Mokelumne Hill where Lambert Beatty
was playing to such poor business that they had to close down.
Beatty and his wife, too proud to let anyone know they were penniless, locked themselves in the scene shop and prepared to starve
to death.

Discovering their plight, Ayers, who had never been onstage
in his life, proposed that he and Beatty make a tour of the sur-
rounding camps with a two-man show of readings and short

    2. H.P. *Davis,* Gold Rush Days in Nevada City *(Nevada City· Berliner &
McGinnis, 1948), p. 59.*
    3. San Joaquin Republican, *December 27, 1854.*

scenes. After fair profits in Campo Seco and Volcano, luck turned against them, and they arrived at Hangtown (later Placerville) as destitute as they had started.

Here they met another pair of stranded actors, the Eldridges, abandoned by their company after a profitless tour of the mines. Mrs. Eldridge was a spirited actress, much admired by the miners.[4] Two years earlier, she had caught their attention by shooting at a man who insulted her. She missed, him, but the action had brought her many admirers.[5] Later, as "Mrs. Mestayer," she would play in touring companies managed by Thorne, by Robinson, by the Chapmans, and by the Bakers. Eventually, she became a successful manager on her own before returning east.

Certain of her popularity, Mrs. Eldridge now proposed the four of them give *Hamlet*. With nothing to lose, they transformed a large hotel room into a temporary stage and, with the help of volunteers, played four nights to houses so crowded that they all went away with full pockets.[6]

A less happy fate befell a Sacramento dancing master infected with the desire to play the Danish prince. In April, 1856, C.C. Clapp somehow convinced the theater manager to let him replace young Edwin Booth, who had been wildly applauded in the role. Booth did not object and even agreed to play the Ghost. The first night went without incident, but when Clapp tried to repeat the experiment, the audience exploded with fury, shouting and stamping until Clapp, stammering and stumbling, forgot his lines. He refused to submit and finished the performance, but he never tried it again.[7] His disappointment was complete when Booth's Hamlet was lavishly rewarded with a barrage of gold a few nights later.[8]

4. *The Placer Times, August 30, 1850,* reviewing her benefit the previous night was "happy to observe" that she was "becoming decidedly a favorite with the audiences of Sacramento," and hoped she would "long grace our stage with her presence." In 1851, her benefit in Nevada City brought her $600.

5. Evening Picayune *April 10, 1852.*

6. *Ayers, 138–142.*

7. *Stanley Kimmel,* The Mad Booths of Maryland *(New York: Bobbs-Merrill, 1940), p. 123.*

8. *San Francisco Theatre Research WPA Project 8386, O.P. 465-03-286, Monograph IX, ed. Lawrence Estavan (San Francisco, August, 1938), pp. 112–113.*

A worse fate was in store for a Mr. Defries in 1859. Lewis Baker was managing San Francisco's American Theater when Defries appeared, announced himself as the best actor in the country and demanded to play Hamlet. He had never actually been onstage, he said, but he demonstrated his talent by reciting a soliloquy — with gestures.

Baker's first thought was simply to show him the door, but Defries' arrogance called for some kind of chastisement. With inspired malice, Baker hired him and, taking the entire American company, the newspapers, and the audience into his confidence, began rehearsals. Defries was treated as the super-actor he claimed to be. The papers heralded his debut with ecstasy, and for a whole week, crowded houses applauded his every speech and gave him unprecedented curtain calls afterwards.

The climax came at his benefit on October 21. As before, the house gave his strutting and gesturing a warm welcome, but when he began "To be or not to be . . ." someone threw an orange. Not in the least ruffled, Defries caught it and proceeded to peel and eat it as he continued the soliloquy. The astonished audience was only momentarily stopped. A few minutes later, a storm of vegetables, accompanied by various uncomplimentary noises, filled the air. Defries stubbornly held his ground until he saw the human mass rise from its seats and head toward him. In a series of leaps he left the stage and the theater, and when last seen was bounding down the street with the entire audience in pursuit. He was never heard of again.[9]

Such demonstrations were not uncommon in cities, but not all amateur performances were disasters. San Francisco and Sacramento, accustomed to the best actors of the day, showed little mercy to amateurs, but the remote camps were kinder, and anyone with a modicum of talent could be fairly sure of an enthusiastic reception. In Deer Creek, Montana, a woman with two children was abandoned by her husband. Known only as "Laura Agnes," her sole connection with the theater had been an actress-mother, but now, threatened by starvation, she put together a few half-remembered bits and pieces and performed *Opera Mad; or*

9. *San Francisco Theatre Research WPA Project 8386, Vol. 3, pp. 67–69.*

*Romeo and Juliet,* in which she danced, sang, and flirted with a dummy Romeo.

Her predicament and her courage touched the softhearted miners, and she became the rage of the Montana camps, playing to crowded houses that showered her with gold — until the night a group of prospectors, drunker and rowdier than usual, playfully carried off her "Romeo" and roughhoused the stuffing out of him. The next morning, as she breakfasted at her hotel, they presented her with the tattered remnants. Going along with the joke, she played an impromptu scene of mourning, complete with tears, that drove the miners, their own eyes moist, from the room. When they had gone, Laura Agnes laughingly finished her meal and waited calmly for the stage coach to the next town. The shame-faced miners returned to the saloon, made up a sizable bag of gold dust, and tossed it into her lap as she rode away.

Few amateurs were as desperate or as adventurous as Laura Agnes. The majority lived in small towns, acting in unpretentious productions for the amusement of their friends. The most endur-ing of these theaters was in Salt Lake City, where Brigham Young strongly supported the drama as an innocent, moral, and highly proper kind of diversion for his people. According to Kenneth Macgowan, this was the first true community theater in America.

The loosely organized Mormon group, which gave its first show in 1848, was soon structured into the Deseret Dramatic Association around 1850, and by 1852 was performing in the com-munity's Social Hall. Simplicity was the keynote. They made their own scenery, costumes and stage properties; all work and materials were donated by those involved. Performances were regular but not frequent, since preparation time had to be excised from daily tasks. By 1856, this had become burdensome, and it was agreed that players should be recompensed, though the stipend was small and not always in cash.

For the most part, the Deseret Dramatic Association gave light comedies. Tragedy, said Young, was too severe for people already leading such harsh lives. Nevertheless, 1856 brought a pro-duction of *Richard III* and one act of *Othello,* both chosen on the premise that people accustomed to reading the Bible should be well qualified to speak Shakespearean lines. The premise was wrong, and the actors were severely criticized. Three years later, the Mechanics' Dramatic Association, a rival group, was only slightly more successful with a complete *Othello* performed at the home of a member who had enthusiastically turned the ground floor of his house into a stage.

This was the end of Mormon Shakespeare until their Salt Lake City Theater opened in 1862. Modeled after London's Drury Lane, it was without question the largest and most beautiful theater outside of San Francisco, and its first season ended with a production of *The Merchant of Venice,* much applauded for its stage effects if not for its acting.

It was clear that Shakespeare had been beyond the powers of the Deseret Dramatic Association, and not until 1863, when the Association began to import professionals, was another production seen. Their initial star was an old friend, Thomas Lyne. Well known as a tragedian in Philadelphia, New York, and St. Louis, Lyne had joined the Mormon church while they were still in Nauvoo but had subsequently left to pursue his acting career. Now, at the age of 56, he returned to set a precedent as the first "Gentile" to appear on Mormon boards. His roles included Richard III and Othello, and he was evidently pleased by his reception, for he rejoined the church and spent the rest of his life in Salt Lake City.

The following year, they imported the prominent British actor George Pauncefort, and his Hamlet, played on Christmas Eve, 1864, was the first in that city. Two weeks later, he premiered *Macbeth,* a lavish production with original music sung by the hundred-voiced Mormon Tabernacle Choir. The music called for an echo effect, provided by an English quartet specially invited for the occasion but unfortunately it was somewhat marred by their pronounced Cockney accents.

Pauncefort, however, was of a vastly different stamp from Thomas Lyne. He either did not know or did not care that the Mormons regarded the theater as a temple of morality. Smoking, drinking, and bad language were banned from its precincts, and actors were expected to lead upright lives. When it was learned that Pauncefort was living openly with Mrs. Bell, his leading lady, Brigham Young boycotted his performances, and Pauncefort was asked to change his ways or leave. Regretfully, Mrs. Bell was returned to her husband. Pauncefort filled his engagement, but he was not invited again. After a varied career as star, supporting player, and itinerant showman, he supposedly ended his days as an Eastern potentate, complete with palace, guards, and a well-stocked harem.[10]

Salt Lake City was happier with Julia Dean Hayne starring in *Macbeth, Romeo and Juliet,* and *Merchant of Venice* in the 1865–66 season. The willowy Julia enchanted the entire city; Brigham Young loaned her his sleigh (afterwards called "Julia's sleigh" and used only on special occasions), the house was full every night, and she was begged to return as often as possible. Even her divorce the following year did not lessen their fervor.

For each star, the Deseret Dramatic Association provided solid support, and performed regularly even when stars were not available. Those with marked talent were encouraged, and at least one national star came from this group — Maude Adams, who received her early training with them and whose mother had been an important player in her own right.

The Western amateurs, like the soldiers who preceded them, did not mark a milestone in theater. Their Shakespearean performances, by and large, used questionable texts and were of low quality. On the other hand, they did no real harm, they gave much pleasure to many people, and they whetted the appetite for a more intimate acquaintance with William Shakespeare.

10. *Walter Leman,* Memories of an Old Actor *(San Francisco: A. Roman, 1886), p. 323.*

# The Stark Family

Actors have never been known for their stability. The nature and conditions of the profession do not attract the phlegmatic or the security minded. On the one hand, the work requires that emotions be freely expressed, often with great intensity; on the other, permanent theaters like the state-supported Comédie-Française are rare, and to work at all, players must frequently move from one company to another.

Because it was difficult to establish lengthy relationships in a given community, actors tended to marry and bring up their children within the profession. While such marriages could face serious stresses if the partners were in different companies or if one career suddenly outstripped the other, most were as stable and long-lasting as more traditional alliances, and at least four such families made a distinct mark on the Gold Rush theater. The first is the Stark family; the other three will be taken up in succeeding chapters.

Sarah Kirby arrived in San Francisco on January 7, 1850, the first authentic leading lady to reach California. At the age of twenty-seven, she was a slender, strong-featured brunette with a commanding stage presence and a dynamic personality. So far, her career had not been distinguished, but she had a good deal of experience, and she was a fine, if temperamental, actress.

After a debut in Boston and four years of playing in touring companies, she went to New York. In 1847, she met and married J. Hudson Kirby.[1] A few months later, they went to England where Sarah studied with Macready while Kirby starred in London until his untimely death in 1848. She returned to the United States, acting under the name Kirby even after her marriage to Mr. Wingard.[2]

By the time they reached San Francisco, she was a capable actress, and her performance in *The Lady of Lyons* was so impressive that Nesbit McCron hired her as his leading lady. She played several roles in his company, including a majestic Elizabeth in *Richard III,* but her quick temper soon led to a furious quarrel with Mrs. McCron and Sarah left them.

She had no trouble finding another place. J.B. Atwater, former manager of the unfortunate Eagle company, engaged her as actress-manager for the Tehama theater in Sacramento. Their season lasted until July, when Atwater returned to the States and the company disbanded. Sarah went to Stockton and opened their new theater in August, but a month later she was back at the Tehama with a new company.

Here she met handsome, Canadian-born James Stark. He had started as a carpenter in Nova Scotia, but a deep love of acting drew him into the theater. He moved to Boston, where his talent prompted a patron to finance three years of study with Macready in England. He acted in London and on the continent, returned to the United States and made a brief debut in New York, then joined a series of touring companies and gradually travelled westward. In March, 1850, after playing Brutus in *Julius Caesar* for Walter Leman's benefit in St. Louis, he headed for California. He and Sarah Kirby had much in common; both had trained with Macready, and both loved Shakespeare.

---

1. *Kirby was much admired for his athletic and convulsive death scene in* Richard III, *and "Wake me up when Kirby dies" became a popular expression on Broadway.*

2. *The name was alternately given as Wingate and Wingered, but although Harvard scholars prefer the former, I have stayed with the spelling used by most Western historians. They were probably married about a year after Kirby's death.*

Meanwhile, back in San Francisco, Thomas Maguire was building his first Jenny Lind. It was small, seating only 600–700, but a jewel of a house, beautifully decorated with white woodwork, deep rose panels, and a great deal of gilt. In October, he hired Stark and Kirby as co-managers. It was a wise choice. Stark was a fine actor, and Sarah Kirby had a genuine talent for management. On October 30, 1850, the Jenny Lind opened with a repertory that included a generous selection of Shakespeare. The first of these, *Othello,* opened on November 5, and made a strong impression:

> Mr. Stark's Othello was a masterly and finished exhibition of the character. It appeared perfectly evident that he is not a copyist or imitator of any model actor; but that he studies with close application of mind the character he undertakes to represent.... He does not, therefore, show us Macready's Othello, or Forrest's but Shakespeare's, and we have never seen what in our judgment, was a truer or more forcible presentation.[3]

It must have been a most effective performance. Stark was so carried away that he stabbed himself painfully in the last act

He had good support as well. The versatile John Hambleton, the beautiful and charming Mrs. Hambleton, and the talented Henry Coad had been professional actors in Australia. Mme. Duprez, "from the Paris and London theater," had already charmed San Franciscans when she first appeared in the summer, and the rest of the company was at least competent.

A promising season was interrupted by tragedy. On November 16, Wingard was killed in a fall from a horse, and Sarah was widowed for the second time. The theater closed for a few days, but she was soon back at work, and their next Shakespeare was ready in a month. *Hamlet,* with Stark in the title role and Sarah as Gertrude, was a triumph, moving a critic to declare the play "never before had such a presentation on Pacific shores."[4] His enthusiasm seems to have blinded him to the fact that, apart from the abbreviated version in Los Angeles three years earlier, this was the first Hamlet "on Pacific shores."

3. Evening Picayune, *November 6, 1850.*
4. Alta California, *December 22, 1850.*

Their repertory ranged through Massinger, Otway, Kotzebue, Sheridan, Bulwer-Lytton, and a host of unknowns, but they always returned to Shakespeare. A thin house for the California premiere of *The Merchant of Venice* on January 4, 1851, was probably due to bad weather and not a lack of interest in Shakespeare, for within the week, six of San Francisco's most prominent businessmen published an open letter urging Stark to give *King Lear*. He promised them a performance on January 18, a rash pledge for so small a company. Even more daring was his announcement that he would perform "the original text," instead of the usual Dryden-Shadwell version with its happy ending.

The commitment could not be kept. Tragedy struck a second time when young Mrs. Hambleton committed suicide. A few hours before the performance of January 14, her husband accused her of having an affair with Henry Coad. There was a fearful row, and he rushed from their hotel room threatening to kill Coad. In despair, Mrs. Hambleton drank a large dose of potassium cyanide which her husband inexplicably kept under their bed.

The theater was dark that night and the next, and a public scandal erupted when Hambleton published a letter charging Sarah Kirby with the responsibility for his wife's suicide. Henry Coad was innocent, he announced. The fault lay with the "fascinating serpent," Sarah Kirby, who had turned his wife against him and encouraged her to leave him. Sarah countercharged that Hambleton had beaten his wife cruelly, a claim others substantiated.

San Francisco was a volatile city where passions quickly boiled into physical violence. With partisans from both sides in the house, Sarah's next appearance on stage presented some danger. The company was severely handicapped by the loss of Hambleton and Coad, Mme. Duprez and Mrs. Mansfield played male roles, visibly reminding the audience of the recent events, and Sarah's entrance was greeted with ominous hisses.[5] As the evening progressed, however, she won them over. Afterwards, she gave her side of the quarrel in a curtain speech, and the night ended with

5. *The play was Richard Sheil's* The Apostate, *and Sarah Kirby played Florinda, the romantic heroine.*

"a regular storm of cheers."[6] Afterwards, Hambleton disappeared (there is some indication he went to Australia), but Coad returned to the company without a stigma on his reputation.

While Sarah Kirby learned the part of Cordelia, which would have been Mrs. Hambleton's, Stark played *Hamlet* twice. They worked hard and fast, and California's first *King Lear* opened on January 25, 1851, to a full house. The next day the *Alta California* apologized for having neither "time nor space" to give an adequate critique of "this wonderful creation," concluding, "We can only say what every one anticipated, that he was entirely successful."

Sarah's hastily rehearsed Cordelia was received less warmly. One critic complained "she did not appreciate the part of the old king's daughter."[7] The audience evidently did not agree, for she was "called for long and loud." She may still have been smarting from the Hambleton affair, for she took no credit to herself, but "with great good taste and with much gallantry thanked the audience for its kindness to Mr. Stark."[8]

Yet the company seemed dogged by misfortune. During the first week of February, Mme. Duprez attempted suicide. Fortunately, she did not succeed, and the matter was hushed up, but clearly the air was tense. Sarah's temper was short; she quarrelled with the actors and peremptorily dismissed Ned Bingham. After leaving the army, Bingham had settled in San Francisco and was one of the first actors hired for the Jenny Lind. Like other civic-minded men, he belonged to a volunteer fire department, and when his fellow firemen heard of his dismissal, they tore up the theater in protest.

Bingham was reengaged and went with the company when they played a two-week season in Stockton late in February. Again they gave *Othello,* but this time Stark played Iago, a performance he repeated to great acclaim when they returned to San Francisco. Apparently the breach between Sarah and Bingham was quite healed, for when she and Stark left for Sacramento, they left Bingham to manage the Jenny Lind. Unfortunately, it burned a few weeks later.

6. Alta California, *January 17, 1851.*
7. Pacific News, *January 26, 1851.*
8. Alta California, *January 26, 1851.*

While Maguire began building his second Jenny Lind, Stark and Kirby played Marysville. At this time little more than a camp, it nonetheless boasted a real theater. Made of canvas-covered wood and decorated with calico, with wooden benches for seats, it was a far cry from Maguire's "little jewel," but it was better than the back room of a saloon. It must have been a relief to return to San Francisco's comparative comfort, but James and Sarah stayed just long enough to open the second Jenny Lind on June 13. They had other plans. The months of constantly working together had developed a close relationship between them and on June 16, 1851, they were married in Sacramento.

The second Jenny Lind burned in the great fire of June 22, and the intrepid Maguire began a third. The Starks reopened the Tehama and played there until the end of July. By now, their reputation was so well established that a tour of the camps brought crowded houses even in tiny Nevada City. While they were away, the Tehama burned, ending any hope of another season in Sacramento.

They returned to San Francisco and learned that Maguire had engaged Junius Brutus Booth, Jr. (called "June" to distinguish him from his famous father) to manage the still unfinished Jenny Lind. They leased the smaller Adelphi and began their new season with a benefit performance of *Hamlet*. The papers sympathetically urged their readers to support Stark, "whose late misfortunes, present excessive labors, and excellent abilities in his profession, entitle him to favor."[9]

*Hamlet* was called a "masterpiece," and their popularity increased. They moved into the elaborate new American Theater, reputed to be the ugliest in California, to act and co-manage with C.F. Thorne. On October 20, the gala opening night featured Stark reading an ode on Shakespeare to a house so overcrowded and boisterous that the theater sank two inches during the evening.

Thorne's repertory leaned heavily on melodrama; the Starks added a bit of class with another Western premiere, David Garrick's adaptation of *Taming of the Shrew,* known in America as *Katharine and Petruchio.* The two couples might have been a formid-

9. Evening Picayune, *September 20, 1851.*

able combination if a quarrel had not broken their association. One night, it seems, young Charlie Thorne, drafted for an infant role and wakened from a sound sleep when his cue came, responded to Sarah's lines with a round of curses that made the audience roar with laughter. She accused Mrs. Thorne of putting him up to it, and the partnership terminated with acerbity on both sides.

Booth invited the Starks over to the Jenny Lind, which thereupon broke out in a rash of Shakespeare. Stark played Othello to Booth's Iago; Sarah was Desdemona and Mrs. Woodward Emilia, and the *Picayune* proclaimed them "four of the best performers upon the California stage."[10] *Hamlet* was repeated, followed by the first West Coast *Macbeth,* which brought raves for the entire cast, while *Lear* so captivated the audience that it was repeated for Stark's benefit. The curse scene brought utter silence, then deafening applause, and a later writer was so moved that he described the interpretation at some length:

> the man is utterly hidden by the character; his face is the face of Lear, to all seeming, and not the face of Stark; his demeanor that of the thunder-stricken Lear. He presents the sublime character as the sad spectacle of a ruined temple, yet majestic in its ruins. . . . Shall we speak of the awful and impressive scene, during the thunder storm, when he nears the verge of madness, and passes imperceptibly over it, so that while one is conscious that he was sane but a moment before, and is mad now, he at the same time knows not when reason took its flight? Shall we speak of his aspect, his expression of wild majesty, when he looked up and bent his eye with steady gaze upon the cloud that was belching forth its thunders? Shall we speak of that touching scene when he recognizes Cordelia? Shall we, in fine, allude to the last and in some repects the best scene of all, when he brings his dead daughter in, with the hangman's rope still about her neck? We know not in what language to describe these scenes; they must be seen to be understood and appreciated.[11]

The day after Christmas, Stark played Iago to Joshua Proctor's Othello, and early in January a benefit for Booth before going

10. Evening Picayune, *December 9, 1851.*
11. Placer Times, *January 19, 1852.*

East to try his luck in New York again. For some reason, Sarah did not accompany him, but the separation was apparently for professional reasons and not a matrimonial rift. While he was gone, she put together the "American Stock Company" and spent the summer playing in Sacramento.

Stark spent most of 1852 in New York without great success, and he returned to San Francisco at the end of the year. He and Sarah engaged the American Theater and in January, 1853, despite a severe cold, they opened a series of Shakespeare plays. *Richard III* and *Hamlet* played to "full and admiring" houses,[12] were followed by *Othello,* again with Joshua Proctor in the title role. Stark's Iago, however, stole the show. He had "improved wonderfully" in the last two years, said the critic,

> The ease with which he assumed the garb of sincerity and friend-ship before Othello, the subtlety with which he undermined Cassio and managed Roderigo, were fine touches, and displayed evident marks of genius. . . . The expression which he assumed during the last scene of Othello, for instance, was perfect; it not only showed the malignant villain, but the villain conscious that his crime was detected, and being detected reckless of any result, and thoroughly satisfied with what he had done.[13]

*The Merchant of Venice* came next. The critic found Shylock less impressive, although Stark's portrayal of the "pinching, revenge-ful" character was considered "truthful." He was clearly a favorite actor, and the overall judgment was gentle. "Mr. Stark plays Shylock about as well as Mr. Booth plays Hamlet. Although both are fine performances yet neither is the highest effort. . . ."

Such remarks suggest a much finer discrimination than had been practiced only the year before. Now the actor is no longer praised simply for knowing his lines, but for his concept and skill. Stark's multileveled Macbeth was fully appreciated, and the reviewer spent some time admiring his interpretation:

> Macbeth was not a weak nor a cowardly man; he was, in reality

12. Golden Era, *January 2, 1853.*
13. Placer Times, *January 4, 1853.*

brave, possessed much of the milk of human kindness, and inclined to be high minded and loyal. But ambition, the supernatural influences of the witches, and the towering mind of his wife, were too much for what strength of mind he had, and he fell in an evil hour. The murder of the King was as a noxious spring which burst forth near where the pure, strong current of his life was flowing on, discharged its waters into that current, and poisoned it forever afterwards. He was a fatalist, feeling that he was driven on by fate, and though fighting against it more and more, conscious as time stole on that he was fighting in vain.[14]

The Shakespeare season was a decided success, and the first full-length *Henry IV, Part I* seen in California played to an overflowing house. Stark's "amiable and brilliant" Falstaff was "masterly," as "blooming and jolly in his hands as Shakespeare himself could have desired." The supporting cast was excellent, and a "thoroughly satisfied" audience gave the players "frequent and unbounded" applause.[15]

Sarah Stark was also admired and considered equally good in comedy and tragedy, but her reviews were uniformly cooler than her husband's. She was consistently praised for her "judgment"; her Portia was "lawyerly," her Katharine "truthful," her Lady Macbeth "a woman of powerful, but ill-balanced mind, ambitious, but by no means devoid of the finer womanly qualities," her Cordelia was "effectually rendered." The words suggest a style perhaps more cerebral than emotional. Although extravagantly praised as a "pioneer of the drama," she was commended more for her management than her acting.

In spite of the rave reviews and the marked affection of their audiences, the Starks were restless. Australia, too, had gold fields, and a rush comparable to California's offered an inviting prospect. At the end of their Shakespeare series and a "Grand Farewell Complimentary Benefit," they set out for Sidney on March 9, 1853.

They were gone for fifteen months, and the venture was, by all accounts, highly profitable. On May 14, 1854, the *Golden Era* reported that Sarah Stark had sent $20,000 to her sister in San

14. Placer Times, *January 15, 1853.*
15. Placer Times, *January 17, 1853.*

Francisco, and when they returned six weeks later, they were variously reported to be between $60,000 and $100,000 richer, a fact not overlooked by the profession. They were not content to rest on golden laurels, however, and by the end of July, they were back onstage at the new Metropolitan Theater.

Stark was an inveterate experimenter in his acting, and during their absence his style had undergone a noticeable change. Not everyone was pleased. When he played Iago to Edwin Booth's Othello, critics complained that his performance was "marred by the indistinctness of his utterance in many of the finest passages — the words blending together as it were, in their passage from his throat."[16] His new Falstaff was judged "good, but not his best."[17] On the other hand, his Lear, played for Sarah Stark's benefit on August 9, was deemed even better than before, and the performance was interrupted time and again by "thunderous applause."[18]

The *Golden Era* unbent enough to call Stark and A.J. Neafie the "only tragedians" and Sarah the "only tragic leading woman" on San Francisco boards,[19] but it was almost a year before the decision was conclusively in his favor. "When he first came," said one writer, "he was of the Macready school . . . his countenance was inexpressive," but now, "having reached the limits" of that school, "he has passed at one leap into the preferable style of nature. . . . With the exception of the elder Booth his superior has not been in California."[20]

But more than Stark's style had changed. The audience too was different. California had seen a swift improvement in the quality of theater, and well trained actors were no longer a rarity. Stark was not the only Shakespearean, he was not even the best; others had the advantage of novelty and variety. Although there was great affection for the Starks, attendance at their performances dwindled, and it was evident their influence had waned. The *Golden Era* claimed it was because their repertory was mainly "threadbare" old plays, "so familiar that every street-boy quotes

16. Wide West, *August 6, 1854.*
17. Golden Era, *August 7, 1854.*
18. Golden Era, *August 13, 1854.*
19. Golden Era, *November 26, 1854.*
20. Pioneer Magazine, *January, 1855.*

them." The charge probably referred to the bulk of their repertory, not Shakespeare, for when they moved to the American Theater in December, they successfully produced a whole series of his plays, including four Western premieres: *King John* starring James as Falconbridge, *The Merry Wives of Windsor*, *A Midsummer Night's Dream*, and the only Western production of *Pericles, Prince of Tyre.*

The altered mood of the town must have affected them, for at the end of the season, they announced they were leaving for Europe. Their departure was planned for the spring, and to fill the intervening days, they visited Sacramento for the first time in three years, ending their season with one more California premiere, *Coriolanus*. Sarah was earnestly congratulated for her strong Volumnia, but once again James was the star, his Coriolanus ranked "among his greatest efforts."[21]

Their departure for the East was postponed again and again. Possibly Stark's health was a problem, for he did not act at all in the spring of 1855. Perhaps their funds were low; Sarah took at least one benefit and acted in several for other actors. She also played supporting roles in several companies, at one point repeating her regal Elizabeth when the young Edwin Booth played *Richard III*.

If Stark was ill, he was sufficiently recovered by June to join Sarah in giving readings in Sacramento and to star in a summer tour of the mining camps. In Nevada City, where actors were always assured of good houses, they played a heavy season that included not only several tragic melodramas but *Macbeth*, *Richard III*, *The Merchant of Venice*, *Henry IV*, and *Hamlet*. Here, the change in his style was favorably noticed, and the local critic marked his Hamlet as "peculiarly his own" and coming "nearer to our idea of what it should be, than any former representation by the different stars of the age."[22]

For the rest of the year, there was no more mention of Europe, or, indeed, any kind of expedition. Sarah took over the management of the San Francisco Union Theater until the end of October,

21. Golden Era, *February 18, 1855.*
22. *Mabel Celeste Ashley,* Gold Rush Theatre in Nevada City, California. *Unpublished Master's thesis (Stanford, 1967), p. 80.*

and James played *Macbeth, Hamlet, King Lear, Katharine and Petruchio, Richard III,* along with his first Wolsey in *Henry VIII* and a benefit performance of *Coriolanus.* The box office receipts did not match the critical acclaim, however, for San Francisco was in the midst of a depression. As audiences grew leaner, they remembered the enormous profits they had made "down under" two years earlier and changed their plans accordingly. After one last performance of *King Lear* on February 5, 1856, they set sail for Australia.

This time they stayed a year and a half, returning to San Francisco in June 1857 to find the theater still doing poorly. Very sensibly, they started off at once on a tour of the mining towns. It was triumph. Sacramento and Marysville cheered the return of a Shakespearean repertory, and they were greeted as old favorites in Placerville, Oroville, Forest City, and Downieville, while a week of packed houses in Nevada City was climaxed by a complimentary benefit for Stark.

But in San Francisco it was clear their second emigration had completed the erosion of their popularity, and even their best offerings could not fill the theater. They ended the season early and announced they were going to "the Atlantic States and England," not to return for several years. How serious they were about staying that length of time is debatable, for they had just bought ten acres of land in San Jose and arranged to have a house built on it during their absence.

Sarah was given a complimentary benefit on November 1, and they left at once. Like most actors, they performed wherever they traveled, but the reviews were mixed. Word came back that their houses were good in New Orleans and St. Louis but poor in Chicago. In New York, where they played *Julius Caesar, Katharine and Petruchio,* and *Hamlet,* they had only an "indifferent success," and they never reached England at all.

They returned to California in August, 1858, and George Ryer promptly invited them to Marysville, where they played to enthusiastic audiences. After New York's cool reception, it must have comforted James to play for old friends who openly regarded him as one of "the greatest living actors." With those words ringing in his ears, he was ready to face San Francisco once more.

In February, 1859, he played Othello at Maguire's Opera

House, but his performance was overshadowed by the Iago of Junius Brutus Booth, Jr. In the spring, he took over the management of the Lyceum theater and brought James Anderson from New York as a special attraction. For five nights of *Hamlet* and three of *Othello,* Stark and Anderson alternated playing the title roles with fair success, but when they attempted *Romeo and Juliet* at the American, they met total disaster. Not even the beloved Alexina Baker as Juliet could save Anderson's "most debased and unnatural" Romeo, and Stark's Mercutio was called only "passable."[23] Whether he realized it or not, the golden days were over.

The Starks moved into their house in San Jose, though they were seldom at home. During the 1859–60 season, they played a series of small towns like San Andreas, Nevada City, Placerville, Los Angeles, and in the summer of 1860, with George Ryer as partner, they played the agricultural fairs in Marysville, Stockton, and Sacramento.

In 1861, the Starks opened Maguire's new Metropolitan Theater but they stayed in San Francisco only a short time. At this point, their lives began to diverge. James was soon back on the road, while Sarah, apparently tired of travelling, settled in San Jose. The separation was complete when James caught "silver fever" during a season in Virginia City in 1862 and left the theater for the even more precarious field of mining. From that time on, he acted only on special occasions. His last performance in San Francisco was on January 27, 1864, a benefit for Sarah. Four years later, they were divorced.

Accounts of their subsequent history vary. Some say James returned to acting and toured, that he went to Australia, that he had a small part in Edwin Booth's famous hundred-night *Hamlet* in 1865. None of these stories is substantiated. On May 11, 1871, a newspaper reported that he had a stroke in Virginia City and was not expected to live, but he must have recovered sufficiently to go East, for he died in New York City on October 12, 1875.

Sarah left off touring but not the theater. In 1863, she co-managed the Metropolitan with Emily Jordan and acted supporting

23. California Spirit of the Times, *May 28, 1859.*

roles. After her divorce from Stark, she married Mr. Gray, a New Yorker, and probably retired from the stage. In 1883, again a widow, she married C.F. Thorne, with whom she had once co-managed the old American Theater, and may have gone to live in New York with him. When he died in 1896, she returned to California and spent the remainder of her life in San Francisco.

In the truest sense of the word, the Starks were pioneers. Into the crude, brawling West of the Gold Rush, they introduced a taste for the best, and they helped mold the standards of the rough new world. If they had not left California for the long visits to Australia, would their names have been better remembered, their stature in California's theater history more exalted? Probably not. They were not giants; Sarah was a better manager than actress, and James somehow lacked the magic of a Booth, a Forrest, or even his master, Macready. But they did introduce more Shakespeare than any other actors, and their performances showed Californians that theater was more than amateur entertainment. If they were not great themselves, they most certainly created a taste for greatness.

# The Chapman Family

By no stretch of the imagination could the Chapmans be considered "pure" Shakespeareans. As managers, they chose to present instead the broad comedies and exaggerated melodramas that were sure to attract audiences, and their rare productions of Shakespeare were usually burlesque versions. As actors, they were quintessential performers who could play anything from the lowest farce to the highest tragedy, and when they did act Shakespeare, they were superb.

Their theatrical lineage went back to the eighteenth century. Thomas Chapman played the Beggar in the first production of Gay's *Beggar's Opera* (1728), and his grandson, William, acted in Garrick's company at Drury Lane. About 1820, William brought his sizable family to America, where they spent the next few years as strolling players. It was a hard life. Rough wilderness settlements had no theaters, and even finding a place to sleep was a problem. The Ohio River inspired a solution, and William bought a boat where they could live as well as work. It became the first showboat in America.

They played a broad repertory of standard works which they adapted to their varied audiences, adding new plays from time to time, while experimenting and developing their own specialties. It was the most thorough training a player could have, and they developed into extremely versatile entertainers, as much at home on the stage as off.

The name "Chapman" appears so often throughout the gold years that it seems as if hundreds of them came to California. Actually only two branches arrived: George and Mary appeared first, then William and Caroline with their sister, Sarah Hamilton, and her family. The two contingents rarely performed on the same stage, but they stayed in close contact with each other.

George and Mary were true strollers, playing popular fare with a generous helping of songs and dances. They probably came overland, for the first record of them appears in Nevada City, where they opened the tiny Jenny Lind Theater on November 20, 1851. The *Nevada City Nugget* called it a "tolerable success," an understatement, for the miners greeted them with riotous delight. A month later, the audience in Columbia tossed buckskin bags of gold dust on the stage, and when those did not make a satisfying sound, threw so much silver that the town suffered a coin shortage for a week. When they finally did move on, 1,000 of Columbia's 1,250 men escorted them to Sonora.

The second set of Chapmans came to California about six months after George and Mary. William B., affectionately known as "Uncle Billy," made his debut in San Francisco on March 15, 1852. A specialist in comic old men and Shakespearean clowns, he was an immediate favorite and remained so throughout his career. It was his "sister," Caroline, however, who captured everyone's heart.[1] Although photographs show her as rather plain, her lustrous dark eyes, her flashing smile, and her animation created an aura of beauty when she acted. Whether she was performing Ophelia or a burlesque of Lola Montez' Spider Dance, a curious radiance seemed to emanate from her. The sparkling personality contrasted sharply with her behavior away from the theater. In private, she was gravely serious, and during her early years in New York, she spent all her free time working in an orphanage.

The Hamiltons were quite overshadowed by Uncle Billy and

---

1. *George D. Ford, in* These Were Actors *(New York: Library, 1955), says Caroline was William B.'s illegitimate daughter.*

Caroline, but they seem to have accepted the disparity without rancor, for the two families acted together almost constantly. In the spring of 1852, they entered June Booth's company at the Jenny Lind and later that summer, when June brought his famous father to California, Sarah Hamilton played opposite Junius Brutus' Macbeth, while her son, William, played Fleance.

All the Chapmans were essentially strollers, and after the elder Booth departed, Uncle Billy took his family on a tour of the mines. On New Year's Day 1853, they opened Sonora's new Phoenix Theater and spent the rest of the winter playing in saloons, barns, and camp tents, becoming legendary figures who appeared out of nowhere and created magic.

Meanwhile, George and Mary ended their tour at Campo Seco's new little theater in October 1852. With winter approaching, they headed for San Francisco, where George teamed up with June Booth to manage San Francisco Hall. One season in the city was apparently enough for the restless pair who preferred the wild enthusiasm of the mining camps, and two weeks after Mary's "brilliant" benefit on February 13, 1853, they departed.

In Marysville, they joined the company managed by Mrs. Eldridge, then calling herself "Annie Mestayer." The repertory included a number of Shakespeare plays, and George no doubt welcomed the chance to play Macbeth. Like many comedians, he loved to act in tragedy, although Shylock brought him infinitely more applause. Whether it was his determination to play tragedy or Annie Mestayer's management, the theater did not prosper, and by December, 1853, salaries were so far in arrears that the Chapmans went back on the road.

Shortly after George and Mary went to Marysville, Uncle Billy's troupe returned to San Francisco. June Booth engaged them for the Jenny Lind company and immediately cast Caroline in *Richard III*, which was to be his brother's debut as a star. He did not think Edwin was experienced enough to surmount mediocrity, and he knew Caroline would provide ideal support. Edwin turned out to be a success, and Caroline's Queen Elizabeth was called "the finest piece of acting she has given in San Francisco."[2]

2. Placer Times, *April 22, 1853.*

A few days later, Edwin had equally solid support for his first Hamlet with Sarah Hamilton as Gertrude, Uncle Billy's "inimitable" First Gravedigger and, above all, Caroline's Ophelia. In spite of the difference in their ages (she was fifteen years his senior), they were perfectly matched, and, for one critic at least, she outshone him.[3]

At the end of spring, 1853, San Francisco Hall closed for its periodic refurbishing. The two Booths relaxed, but the indefatigable Chapmans joined D.G. Robinson at the Adelphi for a burlesque *Richard III* mixed with scenes from Shakespearean comedies. They returned to the San Francisco when it was again habitable, to support Edwin in *The Merchant of Venice* and *Macbeth,* but by now Alexina Baker's company was offering considerable competition with a Shakespeare series at the Adelphi. June's answer was to present Edwin and Caroline in *Romeo and Juliet.* It was a risky undertaking, for Caroline was bound to be compared to the popular Mrs. Baker, but the gamble paid off. Edwin and Caroline were dazzling. June capitalized on their success by putting them together in a *Katharine and Petruchio* which Caroline played "in a style that has never been excelled in this city."[4] The comment carries some weight, for San Francisco had seen at least a dozen others by then. In the *Much Ado about Nothing* which followed, Edwin's habitual melancholy vanished in the incandescent gleam of Caroline's comic genius, and Uncle Billy's Dogberry was hailed as a masterpiece.

At the end of summer, June presented Edmund Pillet, a popular and prominent businessman, in a short season of Shakespeare plays. For an amateur, Pillet was not a bad actor, but he was out of his league in the Jenny Lind company. The papers were kind to his Othello, but Caroline's Desdemona, Edwin's Iago, and even Sarah Hamilton's Emilia won the praises. In *Merchant of Venice,* June Booth's Bassanio, Edwin's Gratiano, Caroline's Portia, and Uncle Billy's Lancelot Gobbo simply eclipsed Pillet's Shylock. *Hamlet* fared even worse. San Francisco had seen many

---

3. *Frederick Ewer,* Alta California, *April 26, 1853, called her "excellent, as always," but said little about Edwin.*

4. Alta California, *July 13, 1853.*

fine Hamlets — Junius Brutus Booth, Edwin, James Stark, and, in the last few weeks, James Murdoch's outstanding interpretation. Not even with the support of all the Chapmans could Pillet compare with the others. He was not booed, but after the tepid reviews he wisely retired from the stage.[5]

After a last performance of *Katharine and Petruchio* in September, Uncle Billy took his "Metropolitan Troupe" on a tour of the mines. By the end of the year, they had reached Stockton where, on New Year's Day, 1854, Caroline was given a complimentary benefit. She must have needed it, for their houses were thin, and the theater closed a week later. Strollers were accustomed to such vicissitudes. They shrugged and headed for Columbia and Sonora where they could always be assured of good houses.

While the Metropolitan Troupe criss-crossed the Sierras, George and Mary settled down to manage the Marysville theater and did very well with light comedies and melodramas until the theater burned to the ground on May 28, 1854. Disheartened by the unexpected disaster, George announced he was leaving the stage to become a farmer. The change of career lasted only until November, when Samuel Colville invited them to play a season in Sacramento.

The engagement was an enormous success. Already beloved by audiences, they became city-wide heroes one night when a nearby hospital caught on fire. George stopped the performance, led his company to the burning building, and they carried the patients back to the theater where Mary wrapped them in the silks and velvets from the stage wardrobe until adequate medical attention arrived. She then went home and wrote an account of the fire for the *Alta California*.[6]

The idea of farming was abandoned, and throughout the next two years George and Mary toured constantly. In Downieville, Jamestown, Chinese Camp, Placerville, Mariposa, Nevada City and Grass Valley, their houses were crowded to capacity. In Calaveras, they performed *al fresco* on the stump of a giant sequoia

---

5. *A few months later, he played a few more times in Hawaii, then returned to his business in San Francisco.*
6. *San Francisco Theatre Research, WPA Project 8386, Vol. 3, p. 86.*

tree, and the forest echoed to cheers. Even the tiny camps along the Kern River flocked to see and reward them. Mary was especially admired: "Her versatility is astonishing," marveled one writer, "In some of the pieces she had several characters to sustain, which in every instance . . . she has done admirably."[7] In 1857, after an outstanding success in Portland, Oregon, they set off on a tour around the world.

Uncle Billy's group also found it difficult to settle. In May, 1854, they paid a brief visit to San Francisco and filled the Metropolitan with a production of *The Rivals,* but they were soon back on the road and did not pause again until they reached Marysville in November. There they opened a new theater managed by Charles King and Frederick Kent, who made a point of starring Caroline. It was a good engagement all around, and for the first time, one of the Hamiltons was singled out when Sarah's son, William, aged eleven, was commended as a promising young actor. They stayed in Marysville for two months, a long time for such gypsies, but by January, 1855, they were back in San Francisco announcing their departure for Australia and Europe.[8]

Whether this was a true plan influenced by George and Mary's trip or just wishful thinking, it did not come to pass. They did travel — but only back to the mines. For a year and a half the Metropolitan Troupe played to full houses in Nevada City, Grass Valley, Auburn, Yankee Jim's, Michigan Bluffs, Todd's Valley, Greenwood Valley, Georgetown, and Coloma. The tour was profitable but exhausting. Uncle Billy was seventy years old; he bought a large family house in Napa Valley and declared he was retiring — though he let it be known he was still available should anyone invite him to perform.

San Francisco did not forget Uncle Billy. He was frequently asked to act his specialties, and on April 26, 1857, the Metropolitan was crowded to capacity for his benefit. That fall, he joined Annette Ince's company when it went to Marysville. Here, on September 27, he was struck down by an unruly horse, and, although the injury did not seem serious at the time, he never

7. Golden Era, *January 7, 1855.*
8. Golden Era, *January 28, 1855.*

recovered. He died November 8, 1857, at his Napa Valley home, "the best Comedian who has ever appeared in this State, and one of the best in the world."[9] The Metropolitan and the American raised over $1,000 with benefits for his family.

Troupers carry on, and the Chapmans could not abandon the stage. George and Mary returned to the United States and played in the East for some time before finally settling in California. Of their twenty-one children, Mary outlived all but three. Their daughters, Mary, Blanche, and Ella, continued the family stage tradition for many years. The Hamiltons acted in small road companies, though none, not even their son William, ever became a star. Uncle Billy's son started well when, as "Master Billy," he played Shylock at the age of ten. Not long after, he garnered the only good reviews when he played Arthur in Julia Dean Haync's 1857 production of *King John,* a role he repeated when James Wallack appeared in it a year later, but he remained a supporting actor all his professional life.

After Uncle Billy's retirement, Caroline confined her acting to San Francisco, occasionally appearing with her nephews and nieces, but more often on her own. In January, 1858, she and Matilda Wood delighted San Franciscans with burlesques of standard plays, but she pleased them equally well when she acted serious roles. Ironically, her name is scarcely known outside of San Francisco, although she might well have become a national star when Dion Boucicault invited her to New York in 1860. She was an immense success, but just as her conquest was nearly complete, she was struck down by a mysterious illness. A rapid weight loss sapped her exuberant energy, and she was soon too weak to finish a performance. Medicine provided no cure, and no treatment seemed to help. Sadly, she returned to San Francisco — but not to the stage. Instead, she turned to the interests of her youth and worked in an orphanage until her death in 1875.

To San Franciscans, she was always "our Caroline," and every town she played felt the same. A story told long after she had left the stage gives evidence of that affection. It seems her nieces, Blanche and Ella, were threatened by highwaymen and, aware of

9. Marysville Herald, *November 9, 1857.*

the charm the Chapman name held, they identified themselves and pleaded for leniency. When the chief of the band demanded proof, they convinced him with songs and dances, and the passengers went free. After they arrived at their destination, the stagecoach driver fainted — he had been sitting on a box of Wells Fargo gold.

The Chapmans introduced no new Shakespeare to California. Their originality was not in innovation but in that area where the theater is most powerful: performance. Their audiences were amused, awed, surprised, and delighted. They did not merely admire the Chapmans, they loved them. Shakespeare could have had no better ambassadors.

# The Baker Family

Like the Starks, the Bakers were a husband and wife team, but the resemblance stops there. They were American actors by birth and by training, their reputations were well established before they came to California, and their arrival in February, 1852, was loudly heralded by the papers. Their respective roles were also reversed; Alexina was the star, Lewis was more manager than actor.

Alexina Fisher Baker was the first genuine star in California, preceding Junius Brutus Booth by six months. Daughter of an acting family, she had been on the stage since early childhood when she played one of the young princes in *Richard III*. A bit later, as a "prodigy," she appeared as Richard himself and as Shylock. A leading lady in New York at fourteen, she was now thirty years old and at the height of her powers. If she wasn't the greatest actress on the American stage, she was by far the best California had seen.

The year before they came west, Alexina married John Lewis Baker, a stage-struck Philadelphian who had acted in many amateur productions but had been a professional for only three years. His diminutive height and his prominent nose kept him from being a leading man, but he handled character roles well and could step into almost any part on short notice. He had taken over

Alexina's career, and his management revealed a sound knowledge
of theater, high standards and, perhaps more important, he knew
how to discipline a company without injuring actors' feelings.

In San Francisco, they played first for June Booth at the Jenny
Lind, beginning February 14, 1852, with Sheridan Knowles' standard vehicle for leading ladies, *The Hunchback.* Critics approved of
Alexina's "freshness" and "finish" in the role of Julia; a week later,
the Western premiere of *Romeo and Juliet* drew rave notices. Her
Juliet, wrote the *Alta California,* was "relieved . . . from the sickly
sentimentality that is given by the majority of actresses" and
presented as "a girl loving and loving deeply." At the curtain call,
the audience showered her with bouquets to one of which was attached a diamond ring, engraved on the inside with the words,
"Auld Lang Syne," a tribute from a homesick Philadelphian.

By now, San Francisco had seen a good deal of fine acting
from the Starks, June Booth, and the Chapmans, but their support, particularly in Shakespeare, was often ragged. Changing
bills every night placed a heavy burden on actors' memories, and
many took refuge in ad-libbing—not always to the author's
benefit. Lewis Baker made sure his wife was surrounded with able
players, insisted they learn their lines, and rehearsed them carefully. The resulting productions were coherent, cohesive, and
uniformly excellent. Alexina's "refined manners" and genteel,
ladylike behavior, in sharp contrast to Sarah Stark's strong
characterizations, enthralled the rowdy miners, and for twenty-
five straight nights, every seat at the Jenny Lind was filled.

Still, the city was not surfeited with them. They added the
Starks to the company and moved to the Adelphi. That theater,
however, was badly in need of renovation, and they soon went
over to the American, where, on March 8, 1852, they gave the
California premiere of *As You Like It.* It was a dark and stormy
night; between the howling of the wind and the drumming of the
rain on the roof, the actors could barely make themselves heard.
Nevertheless, the theater was crowded, and the next day reviewers
found themselves hard pressed to find enough superlatives for
Alexina's Rosalind. The praise for Lewis was more restrained, but
everyone agreed the quality for the production as a whole was
unmatched.

*As You Like It* was quickly followed by *Much Ado about Nothing, Katharine and Petruchio, Othello,* and *The Merchant of Venice,* all of which were greeted rapturously. Apparently their success aroused no animosity in other companies, for not only did the Starks act with them, but June Booth played in their *Macbeth,* although he was then preparing to leave for the East. Three days later, they returned the favor with a farewell benefit for him.

In May, they set off for a tour of the mines and even more enthusiastic audiences. Sacramento adored *As You Like It,* Nevada City considered their *Richard III* and *Romeo and Juliet* the best they had ever seen. Alexina's gracious gentility was a poignant reminder of wives, mothers, and sweethearts, and the sentimental miners poured forth $30,000 worth of gold dust.

When they returned to San Francisco in September, the city was agog over Junius Brutus Booth, Sr. His son, June, had persuaded him to come out for a short season, and he had taken the city by storm. For his final performance, he chose *The Merchant of Venice,* and Alexina, one of the few actresses who could play a Portia not completely overwhelmed by his "savage Shylock," was asked to appear with him. These two stars filled the house to capacity, and the performance was a triumphant climax to Booth's visit.

With June Booth at San Francisco Hall and the Starks at the American, the Bakers again took the less desirable Adelphi. Its tobacco-stained walls and aroma of unwashed bodies did not keep audiences away, but after five extremely profitable months, they closed it for a wholesale airing, cleaning, and repainting.

When they reopened in late February, the Starks were playing a last Shakespeare series before their departure for Australia. The Bakers, perhaps as a gesture of good will, gave no Shakespeare until after the Starks left. On April 6, however, they repeated *Romeo and Juliet,* followed by the West Coast premiere of *Comedy of Errors.* It was a daring experiment with Alexina and her sister, Oceana, in male roles as the two Antipholuses, while Lewis and John Thoman played the two Dromios.[1]

---

1. *This was one of Oceana's rare appearances. Although she too had been a child actress, she seems to have had no taste for the life and as an adult acted only a few times to please her sister. After leaving California, she never went on the stage again.*

Even with redecoration, the Adelphi was unsatisfactory, and on May 7, they moved into the American, where Alexina went back into skirts for *Romeo and Juliet*. At this time, Catherine Sinclair, former wife of Edwin Forrest, had just arrived. Still in the throes of a scandalous divorce, she was trying to make her way as an actress, and the Bakers gave her a helping hand with a production of *London Assurance*, in which Alexina and Catherine alternately played the role of Lady Gay Spanker. Alexina was judged the better of the two, but for some reason (illness or pregnancy), she did not act for the rest of the summer. Sinclair, having proved herself an adequate leading lady, replaced her as Beatrice in *Much Ado about Nothing* and played Queen Katharine to Lewis' Wolsey in his West Coast premiere of *Henry VIII*. The *Placer Times* was cool to the acting but had great praise for the staging.

Lewis closed the American until August, when he reopened it with an imported star, James Murdoch, whom he modestly supported by playing Polonius in Murdoch's *Hamlet*. Murdoch was a splendid actor, and when Alexina returned to the stage as his costar in *Macbeth*, their success was assured. After a series that included productions of *Much Ado about Nothing, Romeo and Juliet, Othello,* and *Katherine and Petruchio*, Murdoch was hailed as a great actor and Alexina an "incomparable artiste."

At the end of October, Murdoch went off to tour the interior, and the Bakers began preparations for their return to the East. Before they left, however, they gave San Francisco a new star, Matilda Heron. In point of fact, they made her a star, for she arrived in San Francisco on Christmas Day, 1853, penniless and quite unknown. She went immediately to the Bakers, who not only took her on faith but offered her a leading role.

The play was another bold experiment, *Romeo and Juliet*, with Alexina as Romeo and Matilda as Juliet. Perhaps it was not as reckless as it might seem. The occasion was bound to be special, since it was Alexina's benefit night and her last appearance in San Francisco. Their judgment proved accurate. On January 2, 1854, the house was crowded, the applause was thunderous, and her fans presented her with a "magnificent diamond magic watch."[2]

2. Marysville Herald, *January 5, 1854.*

In the turmoil, Matilda Heron was quite overlooked, but the Bakers did not forget her. On January 15, the company gave her a benefit with their final performance (minus Alexina). The next day, they sailed upriver for a short and profitable season in Sacramento, but they did not actually leave the state until April 2, and then only after softening the blow by a thoroughly fictitious promise to return in six months.

During the next four years, California newspapers kept track of their every move from Boston to New York, from Philadelphia to New Orleans, from Louisville to Cincinnati. At last, on November 18, 1858, the *Daily California Express* gleefully reported that the Bakers, "among the most brilliant stars of California," would be arriving on the steamer *Golden Gate* and would be "warmly welcomed." San Franciscans had not forgotten them, and on their opening night, every volunteer fireman in Pennsylvania Engine Company No. 12 brought a bouquet to toss on the stage at Alexina's curtain call.

Their second visit lasted several months, beginning with a winter season in Sacramento and a return to San Francisco in the spring. Alexina's popularity increased, although it did not always extend to her fellow players. Lewis brought the Eastern actor James Anderson to star in a Shakespeare series. Alexina was once again extolled for her "fresh, sparkling" Juliet, "replete with originality of conception"; Anderson was roundly condemned.[3]

In 1859, they paid another visit, this time bringing James K. Hackett to play his famous Falstaff in *Henry IV, Part 1* and *Merry Wives of Windsor* and give a few Shakespearean readings. Hackett didn't stay long. Essentially an Easterner, he quickly gathered his loot and left for more familiar territory. Lewis then starred Harry Perry in an engagement that became one of his rare failures. Perry had been brilliant, but by 1860 he was in the last stages of alcoholism and frequently missed performances. Sadly, Lewis and Alexina packed their trunks and went home. It was their last visit to California.

Both of the Bakers had long, successful careers. Lewis continued to manage until his death in 1873. Alexina retired, but her

3. California Spirit of the Times, *May 28, 1859.*

charm was not forgotten, and years later, James Murdoch remembered her with affection:

> by nature ardent and impulsive, and yet sensitive and retiring, as an actress she embodied the poetic ideal of the characters she personated. Whatever criticism may have said of her performances, it must be admitted that she has ever been an earnest and faithful expositor of the sentiment of the author she has illustrated, and has never failed to receive a sympathetic response from her auditors. She enjoys, as she merits, the unqualified admiration of the various communities in which she has lived and acted, reflecting honor upon the profession to which she has so long devoted the labors of an exemplary life.[4]

To which Californians would have said "Amen!"

The Bakers introduced at least four Shakespearean plays to Westerners: *Romeo and Juliet, Comedy of Errors, Much Ado about Nothing,* and *As You Like It*—fewer than the Starks, but certainly a respectable number. Their main contribution, however, was in the quality of their productions. Lewis took as much care of the scenery, costumes, and other visual aspects as he did of the actors. Under his management, plays were not hastily prepared spectacles of under-rehearsed actors but wholly conceived creations in which every detail was important. Their productions pleased audiences as much as Alexina's acting and led to a demand for the same high standards to be observed in other theaters.

4. *James E. Murdoch,* The Stage: or, Recollections of Actors and Acting from an Experience of Fifty Years *(Philadelphia: J.M. Stoddart, 1880), III, 402–403.*

# The Booth Family

The Booth family was a two-generation dynasty. Four of them were actors: three became famous, one infamous. Junius Brutus and Edwin dominated the American stage for half a century, June became a prominent actor-manager in California; history has recorded John Wilkes Booth as the assassin of Abraham Lincoln.

June was a handsome, athletic man with a strong resemblance to his father. Some years earlier, he had married Clementine de Bar of the Eastern acting family, but the marriage had not lasted, and he came west with Harriet Mace, who passed as his wife. They preceded the Bakers by more than six months, arriving on July 20, 1851, with a contract to manage Maguire's second Jenny Lind theater.

That stage burned before they reached San Francisco, and Maguire was already starting an even grander theater which he invited June to manage as soon as it was ready. While waiting, June and Harriet played a short season in Sacramento, and his performances inspired the *Placer Times* to call him a "master of the art." He also collected a company for the new Jenny Lind. His judgment proved to be as excellent as his acting, and many who would become California favorites first appeared under his aegis.

The third Jenny Lind opened on October 4, 1851, and San Franciscans considered it the most beautiful theater in the country. Maguire had spared no expense, either in the imported yellow sandstone of the exterior or in the lavish interior decorations. Four days later, June presented *Othello.* The cast, particularly his Iago, received high marks — except for Othello, played by a Mr. Campbell, who suffered from "an insufficiency of physical development and volume of voice."[1] When the play was repeated in December, June remedied the problem by hiring James Stark for Othello.

*Richard III,* on October 24, 1851, "decidedly the best piece of stage acting we have seen in California," had already been "so frequently seen that, if badly played, it is condemned at once." The critic found Booth's Richard "masterly," at times "fully equal to the greatest masters of the stage," quickly adding, lest he be charged with undiscriminating praise, "The stage death of one or two, however, was a relief."[2]

*Macbeth,* given a month later with "original music," new sets and costumes, fared even better. Everyone, from Booth in the title role down to the supers, was acclaimed, and it was so popular it was repeated three successive times. After the Jenny Lind closed at the end of the season, June played it again for the Bakers' company just before he and Harriet left for the East.

Their visit to "the States" was short and purposeful. June had managed the Jenny Lind well in his first season, had collected a fine company, had offered a variety of good plays, but undoubtedly Maguire had hired him on the assumption that one Booth would attract another to the West Coast. June's mission, then, was to persuade his father to come to San Francisco, and he returned in July with the news that the elder Booth was on his way.

The brilliant, erratic Junius Brutus Booth was the greatest actor of the day. English by birth, he was just twenty-one when he made his London debut as Richard III, and William Godwin predicted he would become a star. In appearance he resembled Edmund Kean, whom he admired so much that he adopted Kean's fiery style and dress. The resemblance to Kean seems to have

1.  Evening Picayune, *October 9, 1851.*
2.  Evening Picayune, *October 25 and 27, 1851.*

blunted his career in England, but it was no handicap in America, where he triumphed from his first appearance in 1821. That time, he stayed only two years, but when he returned in 1827, he bought a farm in Maryland and made it his permanent home.

He was an alcoholic and unstable to the point of madness. He was also a genius who could electrify an audience. Much later, William Winter would suggest his acting "lacked the finish" of Macready or Irving, but had to confess that:

> authentic testimony signifies that the soul he poured into it was awful and terrible; the face, the hands, the posture, the move-ment, — all was incarnate eloquence; and when the lightning of the blue-gray eyes flashed, and the magnificent voice gave out its deep thunder-roll, or pealed forth its sonorous trumpet-notes, the hearts of his hearers were swept away as on the wings of a tempest.[3]

Actors as well as audiences felt the power. James Murdoch, who became a star in his own right, felt it as a young player in *The Iron Chest*. He had just opened the mysterious chest when:

> The heavy hand fell on my shoulder. I turned and there with the pistol held to my head stood Booth glaring like an infuriated demon. Then, for the first time, I comprehended the reality of acting. The fury of that passion-flamed face and the magnetism of the rigid clutch upon my arm paralyzed my muscles, while the scintillating gleam of the terrible eyes, like the green and red flashes of an enraged serpent, fascinated and fixed me spellbound to the spot.[4]

Yet the elder Booth was no mere ranter. He was well educated and a talented linguist who could perform as well in Hebrew or French as in English. He studied his parts carefully and "so il-luminated the obscurities of the text that Shakespeareans wondered with delight at his lucid interpretation of passages which

3. *Quoted in Arthur Hornblow's* A History of the Theatre in America from Its Beginnings to the Present Time *(Philadelphia: Lippincott, 1919), I, 324.*

4. *Quoted in Hornblow, I, 323.*

to them had previously been unintelligible."[5] His Hamlet, seen by
a contemporary, left the impression of "a spiritual melancholy, at
once acute and profound,"[6] suggesting the inspiration for Edwin's
Hamlet a generation later. Murdoch, who knew him well and
whose observations are fairly objective, paid the highest
compliment:

> While possessing and wielding the greatest intellectual power in
> dramatic action, there was . . . a total absence of mere stage-effect
> or professional trickery in Booth's acting. His was "the art which
> concealed the art." His acting, while exciting the most thrilling
> sensations of sympathetic fervor and delight, never suggested a
> thought of the manner in which the actor produced them, and yet
> he left the impression of artistic excellence in all the requirements
> of soul and intellect.[7]

Such was the artist who arrived July 18, 1852, accompanied
by his eighteen-year-old son, Edwin, and George Spear, an actor-
friend. They were a few days late, because the night before they
were to leave New York, Booth and Spear had gone on a drinking
spree and missed the sailing. Young Edwin found them and arranged passage on the next ship. He was accustomed to such
responsibilities, having spent the past four years travelling with his
father, keeping him as sober as possible, protecting him from the
effects of erratic behavior, and easing the bouts of depression.

On July 30, 1852, Junius Brutus opened at the Jenny Lind.
He was an immense success, and on August 14, *Richard III* played
to a capacity house. It was one of his greatest roles, and few who
saw it ever forgot:

> I can . . . see again Booth's quiet entrance from the side as, with
> head bent, he slowly walks down the stage to the footlights with
> that peculiar and abstracted gesture, musingly kicking his sword

5. *Edwin Booth, "Some Words about My Father," in* Actors and Actresses of
Great Britain and the United States *(New York: Cassell, 1886),* II, 100.

6. *Laurence Hutton,* Curiosities of the American Stage *(New York: Harper,
1881), p. 270.*

7. *Murdoch,* II, 176.

which he holds off from him by its sash. Though years have passed since then, I can hear the clank and hear the perfect hush of perhaps three thousand people waiting, (I never saw an actor who could make more of the said hush or wait, and hold the audience in an indescribable, half-delicious, half-irritating suspense) . . . [8]

The tent scene was even more effective:

> From the couch where he had been writhing in the agony of his dreams, from the terror which the palpable images of those whom he had murdered inspired, he rushed forward to the footlights, his face of the ashy hue of death, his limbs trembling, his eyes rolling and gleaming with an unearthly glare, and his whole face and form convulsed with an intense excitement. It was the very acme of acting, if such it can be called, and the deathlike silence of the audience was a higher compliment to the actor, than the long and thundering plaudits that followed the performance. [9]

It would be difficult to top such a moment, yet Booth seems to have done so in a "truly frightful" death scene:

> his eyes, naturally large and piercing, appeared to have greatly increased in size, and fairly gleamed with fire; large drops of perspiration oozed from his forehead, and coursing down his cheeks, mingling with and moistening the ringlets of the wig he usually wore in *Richard*, caused them to adhere to his face, rendering his appearance doubly horrible. The remarkable portrayal of the passions—the despair, hate, grief—. . . has probably never been surpassed. . . [10]

The next night all the Booths played in *Macbeth*, with Junius Brutus as Macbeth, June as Macduff, and Edwin as Malcolm, in a benefit for orphans. The company then set off on the ten-hour trip upriver to Sacramento, where they opened at the American on August 19. It was very nearly a disaster. Audiences were alarmingly

8. *Walt Whitman*, The Boston Herald, *August 16, 1855.*
9. *"The Actor" in Matthews, pp. 104–105.*
10. *H.P. Phelps*, Players of a Century. A Record of the Albany Stage *(Albany: McDonough, 1880), pp. 118–119.*

small, and their income, always precarious, diminished accordingly. The usual explanations — that Sacramento was cruder than
San Francisco, that miners facing real tragedy found their solace
in saloons and could not tolerate Booth's "tortured impersona-
tions" — do not seem adequate.[11] The theater was as healthy in
Sacramento as in San Francisco, and players were constantly shifting from one city to the other. A more likely explanation might be
the time of year. Without the benefit of San Francisco's cooling
sea-breeze, Sacramento's temperatures in August approach and
pass 100 degrees, and none of the theaters had the kind of ventila-
tion system so proudly advertised by Maguire. Moreover,
Sacramento was infested with fleas. The theater was no place to
spend a hot summer night, no matter who was playing.

In any case, all three Booths took benefits before returning to
San Francisco. Junius Brutus took *Brutus,* and it may have been
this performance which Edwin recalled years later in describing his
father's power over an audience. At the moment when Brutus' son,
Titus (played by Edwin), is dying,

> a senseless fellow in front made some rude remark which disturbed
> both audience and actors. Raising his head from off my breast, my
> father, without lapsing from the stern Roman character of judge,
> and with a lightning glance toward the fellow, said "Beware, I am
> the headsman!" It was like a thunder-shock! All in front and on the
> stage seemed paralyzed, until the thunders of applause that broke
> the spell; the scene thenceforward proceeded without interruption,
> and ended, as it should end, in tearful silence.[12]

Edwin took *Venice Preserved* for his benefit and played Jaffeir, a
remarkable choice for a youngster. June selected *Richard III,* giving his father a chance to play his greatest role. After this performance, Junius Brutus, with that strange prescience that was part
of all the Booths, handed Richard's crown to June, saying he would
not need it any more.

11. *Theatre Research WPA Project 8386, O.P. 465-03-286, Monograph IX, pp.
6–7,* and Constance Rourke, Troupers of the Gold Coast; or the Rise of Lotta
Crabtree *(New York: Harcourt, Brace, 1928), pp. 44–45.*
12. *Booth, 104.*

Back in San Francisco, he repeated his previous success. Maguire had sold the Jenny Lind to the city, but at the Adelphi Booth played to packed houses for one more week. The final performance was *The Merchant of Venice* with Alexina Baker as Portia to Booth's Shylock, and an enthusiastic audience almost climbed up on the stage in its excitement. Only the critic Frederick Ewer saw him as "a splendid ruin, magnificent in decay, a man whose days were numbered."[13]

It was the last time his sons saw him act. The next day he sailed for New Orleans, leaving Edwin in June's care. After a last brief season there, he died mysteriously aboard a river steamer on the way home to Maryland.

June Booth joined with George Chapman to manage San Francisco Hall, while Edwin, along with George Spear, who had also stayed behind, went off with Wilmarth Waller's company on a tour of the mines. It was very likely June encouraged the arrangement, hoping to give his brother some practical experience away from family dominion.

If so, it was a rugged training school. Camp theaters were makeshift at best. Rough and Ready's "stage" was the second floor of Downie's Hotel, Grass Valley's a room above a saloon,[14] Nevada City's Dramatic Hall had begun as a barn. Yet June's plan (if plan it was) succeeded admirably. Edwin played only small roles, but he did them well. Of his Laertes in *Hamlet*, the *Nevada Journal* wrote, "We believe we but share the common sentiment in being very partial to Mr. Booth's acting." Edwin's "graceful" Gratiano in *The Merchant of Venice* was an example of "how much a piece may be *acted* when no word is spoken."[15]

The tour was interrupted by the terrible blizzard of 1852, and December found the company stranded in Nevada City, cut off from the outside world by ten-foot snowdrifts. Neither food nor mail could be delivered, and as the actors' funds ran out, they extended themselves to earn enough for meals. Edwin played the banjo in the saloon and, with Gates, took a benefit with excerpts

13. *Quoted by Stanley Kimmel,* The Mad Booths of Maryland *(New York: Bobbs-Merrill, 1940), p. 86.*

14. *Kimmel, p. 97.*

15. *Ashley, p. 49.*

from *Othello* and *Macbeth*. Eventually a few supplies and letters came through, among them one from June telling of his father's death and asking if someone would break the news to Edwin. Aware of his extreme sensitivity, no one wanted to tell him, but George Spear was elected. He took the boy aside, but before he could make the grim announcement Edwin, with the Booth foreknowledge of tragedy, asked quietly, "Spear, is my father dead?"

Ridden with guilt because he had not remained at Junius Brutus' side, Edwin joined a small group of hardy adventurers and walked through the snowdrifts to Marysville, where he borrowed enough to get him to San Francisco and June. There, a letter from their mother urged him to stay with June, and they agreed to follow her wishes.

June was a steady man. Although he never had the fire of his father or brothers, he was a fine actor-manager and an excellent mentor for Edwin, whose career he guided carefully over the next few years. Away from the stage, Edwin was still a teenager, headstrong, a bit unstable, with a tendency to drink too much. He needed a firm hand, and the discipline of the theater provided what June could not.

In the early months of 1853, the Starks were giving a last Shakespeare series before going to Australia. Like the Bakers, June wisely offered no competition beyond a single performance of *Othello* in February, but by staying with a repertory of well-known melodramas and comedies, he made San Francisco Hall the most popular theater in the city.

Some time after the Starks left, the theater's scenic artist, Tench Fairchild, chose *Richard III* for his benefit, asking that Edwin play Richard. June objected. Edwin was too young, too inexperienced. True, he had played supporting parts, had even won some laurels in *The American Fireman* a few weeks earlier, but that did not qualify him for such a difficult role. Fairchild persisted, June gave in, and on April 21, the house was crowded "almost to suffocation," with an expectant audience eagerly anticipating a reincarnation of Junius Brutus Booth.

Edwin took his father's approach: a quiet beginning that slowly built to an intense climax. At first, the audience was disappointed at his "tameness," although they appreciated the "admirably rendered" opening soliloquy and found the scene with Lady Anne "full of grace." In the third act, however, Edwin "warmed up," and by the fourth, it was clear he had triumphed:

> The whole house, whose applause previously appeared to be rather of an encouraging character only, were taken by surprise. . . . When the first moment of surprise was over, a sudden burst of applause came, mingled with shouts such have rarely before resounded within the walls of the theatre . . . and when the curtain went down, the calls were loud and long. . . .[16]

At the age of nineteen, he had proved himself a worthy successor to his father.

Three days later he played his first Hamlet. He still looked like a boy, small and slender, but his pale face, dominated by great dark eyes already shadowed by sadness, gave him unusual maturity. June gave him the best support available: himself as Claudius, George Spear as Polonius, Caroline Chapman as Ophelia, and Uncle Billy as the First Gravedigger. It was not the support, however, but Edwin who stunned the audience:

> We venture to assert, without the fear of contradiction, that never in the history of the drama did such a spectacle present itself as was witnessed last evening, at the San Francisco Theatre. A young man, nineteen years old, appeared in Hamlet, for the first time, and played it in a style of excellence which puts to the blush any attempt in the same character we have seen in California.[17]

Criticism balanced the compliments. Edwin was less polished than his father, he lacked "proper weight and dignity," there was a slight "awkwardness" to his movements, and he was not "letter perfect."[18] Yet in all fairness, the critic wrote, no Hamlet could please everyone. Others had not been perfect, either; the elder Booth's

16. Placer Times, *April 22, 1853.*
17. *This and succeeding quotes in this paragraph are taken from the review in the* Placer Times, *April 26, 1853.*
18. *Edwin evidently learned his Hamlet from his father, a stage version that differed somewhat from standard printed editions.*

broken nose had marred his speech, and Stark had suffered from an "icy coldness." Edwin's "philosophical" Hamlet had great appeal, especially the range of expression:

> With Rosencrantz and Guildenstern on first meeting he was familiar and easy; with the King and Queen he was dignified and filled with sadness. All his grief found vent at "O that this too, too solid flesh would melt." With Horatio, he was a warm and high minded friend; with Ophelia, in the feigned madness, he was nearly impassioned enough, while, at the same time, the "sweet sadness" of love were evident notwithstanding the veil thrown over it.

It was a thorough and thoughtful judgment of his strengths and weaknesses. Edwin may not have reached the stature of a Junius Brutus, but he was far more than a boy standing in his father's shadow.

By now June had sufficient faith in his brother to cast him as leading man for Catherine Sinclair, who had arrived in May, but Sinclair was only a mediocre actress, and Edwin was too inexperienced to rise above her level. *Much Ado about Nothing* wasn't a bad performance, but the *Placer Times* merely noted that his Benedick added "much to the success of the play."

In the summer of 1853, he performed his first Shylock and his first Macbeth to mounting roars of praise. He repeated his Hamlet triumph on June 14, and then, in a burst of inspiration, June paired him with that most versatile of the Chapman clan, Caroline. Their *Romeo and Juliet* was enchanting, their *Katharine and Petruchio* and *Much Ado about Nothing* superb.

In August, 1853, June presented the amateur Edmund Pillet in a series of Shakespeare plays. His Othello was outshone by Edwin's Iago, his Hamlet by Edwin's Laertes, and his Shylock by Edwin's buoyant Gratiano that moved a critic to observe, "We have seldom seen an artist who so fully exhibits that assurance that the actor really means all he says and does."[19]

Pillet was complimented, Booth extolled. True, having a

19. Placer Times, *August 18, 1853.*

famous father and a brother who was a manager had given him an entree to the profession, but without his own remarkable gifts the advantages would have been useless and, in fact, might have worked against him. Expectations are higher for the son of a famous father, and no manager can make an audience respond with enthusiasm. Had Edwin not lived up to the expectations, the audience would have booed him as eagerly as they now applauded.

The next time San Francisco Hall gave *The Merchant of Venice,* Edwin played Shylock to Catherine Sinclair's Portia for his benefit. It was "highly successful" though not perfect, only "giving promise of great future excellence."[20] Meanwhile, the Bakers introduced serious competition when they imported the outstanding Shakespearean actor James Murdoch, and June turned to popular melodramas until Murdoch went on tour in late October. Only then did he offer Dr. Robinson's comic travesty of *Hamlet,* C.F. Thorne in *Othello* (with Edwin as Iago), and Edwin himself in *Richard III* and *Much Ado about Nothing.*

The day before Christmas, 1853, the Metropolitan opened, a magnificent brick structure that surpassed all the other theaters in elegance and would dominate the San Francisco dramatic scene for the next fifteen years. Catherine Sinclair leased it and hired June Booth to manage. Within a week, he hired Murdoch, now returned from touring, to act in *Hamlet* and *Othello.* Since the death of Junius Brutus Booth, Murdoch had become the foremost Hamlet, and Edwin went back to his former role, Laertes. In *Othello,* however, given Iago to play, he held his own with the star.

Edwin continued in the company but did nothing memorable for the next six months. The Starks returned from Australia with such convincing proof of its wealth that in July, Edwin and David Anderson joined Laura Keene's company and sailed for that country. June managed the Metropolitan until September, when he went East to settle a discreet divorce arrangement with Clementine de Bar and make Harriet an honest woman. He returned to San Francisco a month before Edwin.

The younger Booth reached California in April, 1855. He came back penniless, but he had no trouble finding work. Cathe-

20. Placer Times, *September 9, 1853.*

rine Sinclair invited him to play Benedick to her Beatrice at the Metropolitan; in other theaters, he acted in *A Midsummer Night's Dream, Twelfth Night,* and *Comedy of Errors.* By September, June was managing San Francisco Hall again, and there, now reckoned "among the finest" actors on the boards, Edwin played Hamlet once more.[21]

Yet all was not well. He was wild, undisciplined. He and Dave Anderson shared bachelor quarters on the edge of town, where they partied, gambled, rode their horses like madmen, and drank constantly. Sometimes the drinking was evident in his performance, and June worried that he would follow in their father's steps. Still, something kept Edwin from going too far. Catherine Sinclair trusted him enough to choose him for her leading man in a month-long tour of the mines in January, 1856, and in April, Ben Baker took him into his Sacramento company. Here, he acted in *Richard III,* as the Ghost in C.C. Clapp's unfortunate *Hamlet,* and later as Hamlet himself. His drinking increased, and critics remarked on it, warning him to apply himself more seriously if he wanted to advance in the profession.

It should not be forgotten that June, too, was a respected actor, even if he had not inherited Edwin's gifts. When San Francisco Hall closed down,[22] he entered the Metropolitan company, playing Edgar to Stark's Lear, and later, Macduff to McKean Buchanan's Macbeth. He was, however, a better manager, and in May he took over the Union Theater, offering three Shakespearean plays that earned a commendation from the severe critic of *The Wide West,* "In *Hamlet* and *Richard III,* the acting of Edwin, and of both in *Othello,* was meritorious."[23]

June was content to stay in California, but Edwin wanted to go back East. He could not afford it. Money simply slipped through his hands, and he seemed dogged by misfortune. In July, 1856, he joined Ben Moulton's Star Troupe for another tour of the mines that might have given him travel money, but once again chance played him false. A week after the company visited Placer-

21. Golden Era, *June 10, 1855.*
22. *It was torn down in the summer of 1856.*
23. *May 11, 1856.*

ville, the whole town burned; the same thing happened in Georgetown and Diamond Springs, and when they reached Nevada City, not only did the theater burn down the day before they were to open but neighboring Grass Valley went up in flames as well. No matter that almost every mining town burned once a year, Booth became an unwelcome visitor, known as "The Fiery Star," a play on the title of a favorite child-star, Sue Robinson, known as the "Fairy Star." To make matters worse, Moulton, discouraged at the lack of profit, abandoned the company (which included his wife) in Downieville, leaving them with a long walk back to Sacramento.

Fortunately, June and Harriet Booth, along with Dave Anderson, were playing there at the Forrest Theater. Edwin replenished his purse by acting *Hamlet* with them. His drinking was under control now (though it would always be a problem), and Walter Leman, who played the Ghost, remembered it as a brilliant performance. A prophetic critic wrote of Edwin's Hamlet that night, "There is nothing now to hinder his onward march to the highest distinction in his profession."[24]

Two benefits in Sacramento and one in San Francisco gave him more than enough for his passage home. The last benefit was a splendid climax to his California years, and his first *Lear* took the audience by storm. Frederick Ewer, who had sternly reproved Edwin for drinking and careless performances, called it "a triumph of art, and a triumph of which any actor on the stage might well be proud." Mr. Booth, he concluded, "throughout the whole performance exhibited more enlarged powers as an actor than we have ever given him credit for."[25] At the curtain, he was called out again and again, and when, at the last call, he pulled off his white wig and beard, even those who knew him well gasped at the youthful face.

He had not yet reached his twenty-third birthday.

The next day he sailed for Panama and home, not to return for more than thirty years. He had finished his apprenticeship, he was ready to take his rightful place as a full-fledged star. The next

24. Leman, *p. 280.*
25. Daily Alta California, *September 8, 1856.*

time he came to San Francisco, he would be the most famous actor in America, his Hamlet the prototype for two generations of players, but his eyes would carry the permanent shadow of tragedy: the death of his beloved first wife, the madness of his second, and, darkest of all, his brother's assassination of Lincoln.

June finished his season in Sacramento and came back to San Francisco. Except for a brief visit to the East in February, 1857, he spent the next seven years in California. A genial, pleasant man and a reliable player, he was always a welcome addition to any company. He never reached stardom, but he provided solid support for stars like Alexina Baker, James Murdoch, Annette Ince, and James Wallack, Jr. He played in several small touring companies and occasionally managed, but after the death of his wife, Harriet, in August, 1859, his name no longer appears in theatrical records. In 1864, he took their daughter Marion to New York. He never came back.

The Booths did not, like the Starks and Bakers, introduce any Shakespeare to the West. Their contribution lay in the excellence of performance. Those who saw Junius Brutus Booth in his brief, dazzling sojourn, never forgot the electrifying experience. Young Edwin not only learned his craft but clearly manifested the greatness to come. June, outshone onstage by father and brother, stood on his own in management, and his taste and judgment gave San Francisco some of the best and brightest Shakespeare it would ever know.

# Stars — More or Less

Shakespearean stars were men. The great tragedies, written for the all-male Globe company, are structured around heroes, and rich as the women's characters are, none compares in size or scope with Hamlet, Macbeth, Othello, Richard III, or Lear. Even when the major roles are relatively balanced, as in *Antony and Cleopatra* or *Romeo and Juliet,* the burden of the play does not rest solely on the heroine. Male stars could travel from company to company without concern for their support, for the stature of an Othello does not depend on his Desdemona. The reverse, however, is not true, and even a great Juliet needs a good Romeo.

Like their celestial namesakes, stars varied in magnitude, but without exception they stood, glittering and unreachable, high in the theatrical cosmos. Lesser performers might rely on the affection they aroused, but stars inspired admiration that sometimes bordered on awe. While the spectrum of stellar personalities included all kinds of specialists, dramatic stars had to be versatile, playing everything from romantic heroes to the wildest farce. In the end, however, they were measured by their interpretations of Shakespeare and, most particularly, the tragedies.

Eastern stars, accustomed to the support of established theaters, generally arrived alone. From Boston to New Orleans, almost every town of any size had a company of resident actors who spent most of their professional lives performing the standard repertory. The visiting star had only to provide his own costumes and personal stage properties, the theater supplied the rest.

In the West, the situation was vastly different. Actors were engaged for a "season" which sometimes lasted only two or three weeks. When they were "at liberty," they usually travelled the mining circuit and, like the prospectors they entertained, shifted from place to place with astonishing rapidity. Such mobility presented at least two problems for visiting stars: without a stable resident company and its standard repertory, their choice of plays was restricted to the most commonly known texts, while good supporting actors were apt to be off touring the mines just when most wanted. There were, however, compensations. All actors were familiar with Shakespeare, and stars, well aware of their own drawing power, paid little attention to the quality of their support. Somehow a cast could always be assembled at very short notice.

The West offered stars positive advantages as well. Grateful for any entertainment, it treated actors very well, and the investment of time required for a visit paid off handsomely in applause and profits. Whether a player was part of the Eastern galaxy or not, he was given a chance to prove himself, and if he succeeded, he became a part of the new galaxy in the West.

Major stars like Junius Brutus Booth were extremely rare in the early days. More common were those who, like James Stark, had some reputation in the East but rose to true stardom in California. Among the earliest of these was Joshua Proctor, who followed Stark by a year, arriving in California in August, 1851. Well known in the Southern states as a strong, capable tragedian, he made his San Francisco debut in *Macbeth*.

The papers merely noted the performance, but in December, Stark, then managing the American, invited Proctor and his actress-wife into the company. Again Proctor played Macbeth, and this time, the critics noticed him. His concept was "admirable," they said, but his pauses were too long.[1] On the whole, they preferred Stark's version.

---

1. Evening Picayune, *December 25, 1851.*

San Franciscans were loyal to their favorites. In *Othello,* Stark won paragraphs of praise for Iago, while Proctor's Moor was merely noted as "excellent." Clearly, he was not a serious rival to Stark's eminence. Yet there seems to have been no ill feeling between them, perhaps because the gold circuit's richer rewards beckoned. After a benefit at the end of January, 1852, Proctor went to Stockton and spent most of the year touring the mines. When he returned to the city, he took over the management of the American and repaid Stark's earlier favor by presenting him in a series of Shakespeare plays.

At this point, the Starks were about to leave for Australia, and, although as manager, Proctor had the choice of roles, he chose to support his star. San Francisco liked that and rewarded him with warm commendations. In *Merchant of Venice,* his Antonio and his wife's Nerissa were given "special notice,"[2] his Richmond to Stark's Richard III was admired, his Macduff received "many approbations from the audience," and his Hotspur, though not comparable to Stark's Falstaff, was complimented as a "faithful rendering."[3] In *King Lear,* the approval was unqualified. After a panegyric about Stark's Lear, the critic concluded:

> We cannot close without alluding to Mr. Proctor's Edgar. It was a most admirable piece of acting, and we have never seen the "Tom's a'cold," and, in fact, the whole scene of feigned madness, rendered better.[4]

By the end of February, he had become a "favorite actor,"[5] and after the Starks' departure, his Macbeth, with Mrs. Woodward as his lady, was unconditionally approved.

Once more he left San Francisco to spend a year touring the mines part of the time, managing the theater in Marysville for the rest. He returned for a brief but conspicuous success with the Bakers in 1854, but the lure of profits to be made in the mining camps was strong, and he soon set out again. By now he had

2. Placer Times, *January 5, 1853.*
3. Placer Times, *January 15 and 17, 1853.*
4. Placer Times, *January 18, 1853.*
5. Golden Era, *February 27, 1853.*

developed a considerable following, and when he left for the East in February, 1855, he was not only a California star but a rich one as well.

While Proctor was making his fortune, another California star was also rising. American-born Wilmarth Waller trained and made his stage debut in Dublin. In 1851, he returned to New York with his bride, a young singer, and played Hamlet at the Broadway Theater. A few years earlier, he would have built his reputation on the East Coast, but by this time the West promised richer rewards. Almost at once, Waller joined the flood of actors rushing to California.

Like the Chapmans, he may have come overland, for his first review is from Nevada City, starring as *Othello* in a company Ned Bingham had gathered in July, 1852. Three months later, he had visited San Francisco, collected his own troupe and was touring the camps. It was a sizable assembly for such a venture: fifteen people besides Waller and his wife. Among them was young Edwin Booth in his first engagement away from his family.

By October, they had reached Nevada City again, where Waller's resonant voice was heard in *Hamlet.* The reviewer, who had seen Macready, Forrest, and Stark, was deeply impressed:

> No rant, no tameness, now fiery with appropriate passion, now subdued to gentle melancholy.... We look upon Mr. Waller's Hamlet as a complete triumph of the dramatic art.[6]

Waller's troupe toured the rough mining camps throughout the fall. Their Shakespeare repertory was small — *Othello, Hamlet,* and *Merchant of Venice* — but, supplemented with a few standard melodramas and comedies, enough to fill houses if the visits were short. The winter of 1852, however, was catastrophic. A tremendous blizzard struck, and they were snowbound in Nevada City. Their repertory exhausted, they gave scenes from every play they knew, they entertained with specialties, Mrs. Waller (who had trained for grand opera) sang arias, Edwin played the banjo. Their struggles were fruitless. No food supplies could get through the drifts even if there had been money to pay for it.

6. *Ashley, p. 49.*

When the mail finally reached them, it brought the news of Junius Brutus Booth's death, and Edwin left for San Francisco at once. The rest stayed with Waller, and when the weather relented, continued their travels. In the later spring, they returned to Nevada City where the long ordeal had created a kinship with the company. They were greeted as old friends, and on May 19, 1853, the theater was crowded to bursting for Waller's last Hamlet.

He stayed in California only a few more months. On July 1, 1853, he opened Craycroft's new theater in Downieville, but the prospect of another mountain winter must have been too much to face. At the end of summer, he left for the East and did not return. He never became a star or even approached the reputation his young protégé, Edwin Booth, would achieve, but as one of the first fine Shakespearean actors, Waller left his mark on the West. For many years, men living in rude towns and primitive tent villages remembered and savored the few brief hours when, thanks to Waller, they tasted the pleasures of civilization.

Unlike Waller, James Murdoch was invited to the West. A rare combination of scholar and actor, he was famous for his beautiful voice, dignified stage presence, and polished style. Born in Philadelphia in 1811, he played in amateur theater there until 1833, when he made his professional debut as Romeo in Albany, New York. Handsome and graceful, he was not an intuitive actor but relied on close study and intense application, and was sometimes considered a bit cold. Nevertheless, his elegance and his intelligent interpretations charmed audiences:

> His recitation is considered to be one of the most easy, natural, and effective of which our stage can boast.... He is clear and remarkably distinct in his articulation, correct and spirited in his gesture, and a perfect master in the delineation of the passions.[7]

Just as he had become well established, both life and career were threatened in 1841 when he accidentally swallowed arsenic, permanently damaging his health. He used his enforced withdrawal from the stage to study and develop his technique, and

---

7. T. *Allston Brown,* History of the American Stage *(New York: Dick and Fitzgerald, 1870), "James Murdoch."*

when he returned to acting two years later, *Hamlet* so struck New Yorkers that it made him a major star.

His health remained poor, and when the Bakers invited him to San Francisco in 1853, his brother, Dr. Samuel Murdoch, insisted on accompanying him as medical advisor. The Bakers gave a good deal of publicity to his first appearance. On August 22, when he opened in *Hamlet,* the American was packed, and many had to be turned away. Cries of "that voice again" heralded his first words, followed by several minutes of applause.

Some of the critics were less enchanted. The *Placer Times,* reflecting a certain loyalty to James Stark, admitted Murdoch's declamation was "elegant," but quibbled with his pronunciation and concluded, "Although there were very many excellencies about his performance, we must confess we have seen the part rendered quite as well before in California."[8] The *Alta California* was disappointed by the first act but thought the rest of the play "the most perfect piece of acting that we have had on the California stage."

> Mr. Murdoch's person, voice, address and bearing were all with the part he played, while his thorough conception and almost faultless reading made his personation a tower of strength.... Through all the varied range of passion, amid the abrupt changes and transitions incidental to the part . . . his action was as finished, appropriate and graceful as the speech which it aided and adorned."[9]

His second appearance as Hamlet was slightly marred by hoarseness, but his Romeo "sustained the reputation that he here previously earned, as a chaste and correct delineator of character in the highest walk of the drama."[10]

With Alexina Baker as his leading lady, he was much admired in *Macbeth* and *Othello,* but his forte was comedy. He delighted audiences in *Katharine and Petruchio,* and in *Much Ado about Nothing*

8.  Placer Times, *August 23, 1853.*
9.  Alta California, *August 23, 1853.*
10. Alta California, *October 6, 1853.*

special note was made that "the sharp passages of wit between them were admirably given."[11]

His engagement ended, Murdoch felt well enough to tour the interior in late November. The tour began propitiously with a wildly successful engagement in Sacramento, but once it was ended, everything went into reverse: the weather was bad, the company poorly trained, and in Marysville he played to almost empty houses. The engagement was only a temporary disappointment. In all the other towns, he was greeted with hordes of ardent admirers, and in Stockton, even the window casements were requisitioned for seating. Their papers mocked Marysville so severely that at last its *Evening Herald* felt obliged to publish a long defense, insisting that people had stayed away because of the inferior company,

> We doubt not that our people will, before long, have the pleasure of again seeing Mr. Murdoch upon our boards, when, with a proper support, he can show us himself as he really is. When this occurs, Mr. Murdoch will see that Marysville is not behind her sister cities in appreciating and rewarding talent.[12]

It was not to be for several months. Murdoch suffered a recurrence of ill health, and his brother Samuel advised him to cut the tour short. They returned to San Francisco late in December.

By that time, Catherine Sinclair had become the manager of Maguire's newest theater, the Metropolitan, the first theater in San Francisco to be lit with gas and, like its predecessors, "sumptuously furnished." Here, on December 29, 1854, she staged *Hamlet* with Murdoch as the star, herself as Ophelia, and Edwin Booth as Laertes. The next day Murdoch played Othello to Edwin's Iago. Both received the highest praise. The papers called him "glorious Murdoch," and applauded his refusal to use a real Bible in *Hamlet* because it had to be thrown on the floor.

On January 15, he ended the Metropolitan engagement and announced that henceforth he would only give readings from Shakespeare. He took his readings on tour and again met with

11. Alta California, *October 19, 1853.*
12. *December 16, 1853.*

solid approval in Stockton and the camps, but again illness ended his travels. By March, he was on the way to recovery and on April 24 was well enough to try Marysville again. The visit was a reprise of the first. The play was one of Murdoch's best comedies, Bulwer-Lytton's *Money,* but the other actors had not learned their lines, and the paper remarked sourly, "we regard it as high treason against good taste to bring this piece on the stage with so many of the personages imperfect."[13] One week later, Murdoch left Marysville for the last time.

Illness prevented his early return to the East, and for two months he rested in San Francisco, exerting himself only to read Shakespeare for the Ladies' Aid Society. In July, Catherine Sinclair gave *Much Ado about Nothing* as a gala farewell benefit for him and played Beatrice to his Benedick. The Metropolitan was full to bursting that night, and with San Francisco's praises ringing in his ears, he sailed for home. In his ten months in California, he had played 100 nights — not a bad achievement for an invalid.

Murdoch never visited California again. The following year, he went to England, where he played until the beginning of the Civil War, when he returned to enlist in the Union army. At the end of the war, he retired to his farm in Ohio to write his memoirs and lecture on Shakespeare, acting only on rare occasions.

The gap left by Murdoch's departure was quickly filled by a star who arrived without fanfare, gleamed brightly for a few short months and then vanished. J.A. Neafie was born in Philadelphia in 1809, began his stage career while still in his teens, and his New York debut in 1838 established him at the top level of his profession. For the next fourteen years, he was popular not only on the East Coast but in the Southern states where he frequently toured.

His best roles were Shylock, Othello, and Richard III, but in San Francisco he chose to appear first in Macbeth. The time was August 1854, a slow season for actors, and houses were poor. Neafie did not wait for them to improve but set off at once for the prosperous mining camps. Oddly enough, his experience was exactly the opposite of Murdoch's: Sacramento received him with marked coolness, Marysville loved him.

---

13. Marysville Herald, *April 24, 1854.*

1. Junius Brutus Booth as Richard III.

*Top*: 11. Ellen Bateman as Richard III. *Bottom*: 12. Kate Bateman as Richmond.

13. Charles Couldock as Iago.

14. James K. Hackett as Falstaff.

The rest of the tour gave him such a reputation that when he returned to San Francisco in November, the *Golden Era* declared Neafie and James Stark the only two tragedians worth watching. He stayed in San Francisco, managing the American theater until the end of February 1855, but in March, he left to star in Estelle Potter's company at Sacramento. This time, he was much admired, but the economy was still in a slump, and houses were poor. The theater closed in April, and one writer, perhaps referring to Neafie, remarked:

> Distinguished actors and actresses visit California, expecting to accumulate a fortune within a few months, but the time has passed when any member of the theatrical profession can become rich in this State in a brief period.[14]

Neafie went to Marysville and played one more month in Potter's company, but again the profits were small. In May, 1855, he returned permanently to the East.

One of the more iridescent luminaries arrived a few months later. McKean ("Buck") Buchanan, second cousin of President James Buchanan and trained in the family naval tradition, began as an amateur actor in New Orleans. After three years as a midshipman and nine more as a cotton broker, he decided his real vocation was the stage. His first appearance in New Orleans in 1848 was a fiasco. He was called "a bad imitation of Forrest," and it was said the only thing he could play was draw poker.[15] Such comments did not discourage Buchanan, and he persevered. Over the next few years, he developed the energetic and boisterous style that became identified with him.

In September 1855, he made his San Francisco debut, playing Othello to James Stark's Iago. Stark, as usual, garnered most of the applause, but Buchanan was not entirely overshadowed:

> we could not but be struck with the profound sensation produced by Mr. Buchanan's rendition of the Moor. There was about it an

14. Golden Era, *April 29, 1855.*
15. *Phelps, pp. 262–263.*

originality—or we may say a peculiarity—which belongs to Mr.
Buchanan, and has won for him so many and such ardent
admirers.[16]

His Macbeth was also considered "of great merit," although this
time with some reservations. He spoke too quickly to be
understood, the critic complained, and,

> In his desire to give emphasis to expression, he indulges too much
> in the deep guttural prelude, which comes forth like a moan....
> These defects are, however, amply made up in his rendition of the
> more striking portions of the character in which he develops all
> the genius of a finished tragedian.[17]

Yet Catherine Sinclair had enough confidence in Buchanan to
engage him for a season that included *Richard III, Merchant of
Venice, King Lear,* and *Othello,* concluding with a bravura *Hamlet.*

In January, 1856, Buchanan took his Hamlet to Nevada City,
but its critic found his interpretation "too robust" and objected to
his "innovations" in the text. A month later, back in San Francisco,
he repeated *Macbeth* with Sarah Stark as Lady Macbeth and Edwin
Booth as Macduff. The Metropolitan advertised it "with new
scenery and dresses ... put upon the stage in a style never before
attempted in California."[18] With Buchanan in the title role, the
advertisement was not overstated.

It was soon clear that San Francisco also preferred the polished
performances of the Booths, the Bakers, and Murdoch. Buchanan
took the logical step, and raised a company for a tour of the camps.
In March, they played Sacramento, in April, Nevada City, and on
May 13, 1856, they set out for Folsom to play forty towns in six
weeks, stopping in such metropolitan centers as Yankee Jim's,
Cherokee Flat, Rough and Ready, Rattlesnake, Mud Springs,
Red Dog, and Fiddletown.

Showmanship was Buchanan's trademark. The ten actors and
their baggage traveled in a carriage pulled by four horses. The

16. Placer Times, *September 9, 1855.*
17. Placer Times, *September 21, 1855.*
18. Placer Times, *February 5, 1856.*

sides of the carriage were adorned with posters announcing that "the finest artists on the Pacific Coast" would perform dramas that had never before been seen and "would never be seen again." At the edge of each town, Buck brought out a huge drum and thumped it all the way to the hotel. Walter Leman, who was the character man on the tour, once remonstrated with Buchanan for being so undignified. His answer was typical, "When the miners see me beating the drum they'll say 'See there's Buchanan, the great tragedian, beating the drum; how odd! it shows that, great actor as he is, he can descend from his pedestal. Let's all go and see him tonight.'"[19]

The countryside was rugged, and the carriage could not be used on mountain trails. In such places they walked, and their baggage was sent ahead on muleback, but even that was not always a reliable course. On one trip, the mules had just reached the crest of a hill when they were startled. Down they bolted, scattering costumes from top to bottom. The accident occurred in late afternoon, and the distressed actors did not reach the town until almost nightfall. A less determined leader might have given up the idea of performing that night, but the man who swaggered through Macbeth in semi–Western costume complete with slouch hat, long black cape and yellow gauntlets was not defeated by a chance mishap. Buck sent a local man up the mountainside to collect their gear, put together a few blankets for a backdrop, and explained the situation to the audience. The show went on, and afterwards he won enough at poker to repair the damages.

The loss of costumes would have presented more serious problems than did the improvised stage. Buchanan's actors were used to makeshift playing areas. In one town they had to play on two billiard tables, making less-than-dramatic exits through a second floor window and down a ladder, and more than once the lack of space resulted in Bosworth Field being knocked to bits in the last act of *Richard III*.

Even in larger towns conditions were rarely ideal. Placerville's theater required actors to play around a large square post directly in the center of the stage. Everyone complained but Buchanan,

19. *Leman, p. 263.*

who made it into an asset in the last act of *Merchant of Venice* by seiz-
ing hold of it on Shylock's line:

> Nay, take my life and all,
> You take my house, when you do take the *prop*
> That doth sustain my house.[20]

They had problems other than space. In Forest Hill's cloth-
and-paper hotel, the curtain stuck, and when Buchanan jerked it
impatiently, one of the kerosene lamps crashed down with it. The
danger of fire was real and immediate—three hundred people were
on the third floor with only one narrow and shaky stairway for escape. Paralyzed with fear, no one moved, and if a quick-thinking
actor had not grabbed the lamp and extinguished it, few would
have survived.

In spite of—or perhaps because of—his posturing and
thundering, Buchanan drew good houses, and the tour concluded
profitably for all. Rather than face San Francisco again, Buck took
his gold and headed for Australia. In February, 1857, the *Golden
Era* reported gleefully (though without support) that his Australian
houses were poor. Whether or not it was true, he soon left for New
York, bypassing California completely.

On his return to California in 1861, he was accompanied by
his daughter, Virginia, and they played a long engagement in
Sonora. For closing night there, on December 23, they gave the
second act of *Romeo and Juliet,* the third act of *Hamlet,* and the second
act of *Richard III* followed by a farce. At the end of the evening,
they were showered with gifts and gold.[21]

Although travel conditions were still precarious, they toured
the mining towns. Buchanan was caught by the great flood of
1861–62 and barely saved himself by clinging to the branches of a
tree until help arrived. The papers took due note:

> McKean Buchanan who was recently "treed" by the sudden rise
> of the waters on the Merced, it appears met with an unfortunate
> loss of "properties," which, it is to be feared, he will find it difficult
> to replace. It appears that while hibernating among the branches

20. *Leman, p. 262.*
21. *Edna Bryan Buckbee,* The Saga of Old Tuolumne (New York: Press of
the Pioneers, 1935), p. 373.

he lost his sword, which has never been heard from since, and his drum, breaking loose from its moorings, floated twelve miles before it came to anchor again.[22]

He recovered enough to continue, and on July 5, 1862, he and his daughter unofficially opened the Topliffe Theater in Virginia City with readings from Shakespeare.[23]

A bit later that year, he organized a full company for another tour. What began as a short trip ended as a highly successful season of several months, mostly spent in Sacramento. The only cloud was a strange antipathy that developed between Buchanan and W.C. Forbes. Usually Buck's actors were congenial, but this time the friction developed into a confrontation one evening when Forbes walked onstage and informed the audience of his grievances. Buchanan thereupon entered from the other side and did the same. The charges grew louder and hotter while the audience, who knew and cared nothing about any of them, was amused and applauded each speaker equally. At last exhausted, the two fell silent, and Walter Leman, who was in the company, took advantage of the pause to announce the farce for the evening — *Family Jars*. Audience and actors exploded into laughter, and the breach was healed.

Buchanan stayed in Sacramento through the winter, but when the weather grew warmer he was back on the road. In the summer of 1863, he gave Virginia City an exceptional *Macbeth* and *Othello*. His co-star was the fine actor Charles Pope whom he admired so much that he hired him for the 1863–64 season at San Francisco's Metropolitan.

Buchanan's management of the Metropolitan that winter ended his last visit on a high note. At the close of that season, he and Virginia went to New York and on to Europe and England, where he played a record 126 straight nights of Shakespeare. On his return to the United States, he restricted his tours to the East and South.

Temperamental, quick to anger, vehement and rash in speech,

22. Grass Valley National, *February 13, 1862.*
23. *It was officially opened by the Starks on July 26, 1862. Watson, p. 91.*

he offended many, and they let him know it. When word first came back that he was popular in Philadelphia, the *Golden Era* retorted, "Humbug!" and when it was rumored he claimed to have earned $20,000 in California, the answer was a pointed, "How this world is given to lying!"[24]

Buchanan was a colorful figure and it was easy for the sophisticated to ridicule him, but the miners found no fault with his larger than life characterizations which matched their perceptions of themselves. He was sensible enough to surround himself with good people, and for all his Barnum-like qualities, he put on a good show. Leman probably summed him up best:

> a man of peculiar temperament; but with a deal of vanity and egotism, and a disposition at times to be overbearing, he nevertheless had true and noble characteristics. I always found in him inflexible integrity and honesty. I think his judgment was faulty, for most certainly he thought himself a great actor; but he is, by no means, the only actor whose judgment is misled by his self-esteem. If he could have curbed his dramatic Pegasus within reasonable bounds, he would have appeared better upon the stage; but his steed always ran away with him.[25]

While Buchanan was touring Australia, John Edwin McDonough, another Philadelphian, made his California debut at the Metropolitan in February 1857. He had been a Shakespearean star for over ten years, and his repertory included *Othello, Richard III,* and *Hamlet,* but his San Francisco reviews were mixed; critics like him and called him "a genius beyond his modest pretensions,"[26] but Shakespeare was beginning to pall. Seven years of constant repetition had bred a cavalier familiarity with his work. "There is hardly a butcher or a newspaper boy in the city who does not understand 'like a book,' the majority of the playable plays of Shakespeare, so often have they seen them acted, ranted, or slaughtered upon our boards," said one writer, concluding that 86

24. Golden Era, *March 7, 1858.*
25. *Leman, p. 265.*
26. Golden Era, *February 8, 1857.*

Hamlets, 63 Richards, and 57 Macbeths were "enough in all conscience to last us the next quarter of a century to come."[27]

Although the complaints were against Shakespeare, it seems clear that McDonough was merely a victim of the growing sophistication in the West. In the last seven years, standards had gradually grown more rigorous, and audiences had not only developed strong opinions about theatrical matters but were loyal to those they knew. Eastern players could no longer rely on their names to draw uncritical houses; regardless of their reputations, they were strangers and therefore suspect.

A month of adverse comments was enough. In March, McDonough played his repertory with Sacramento's "shaky" company and then toured. Marysville liked him well enough but compared him to Buchanan and called him a "frightful hollerer." Smaller towns like Stockton and Calaveras were less critical, but when he returned to San Francisco in June, his success was muted.

He appeared with the star, Julia Dean Hayne, and had excellent support, but his Wolsey in *Henry VIII* was criticized for its "extreme old age" and "boisterous declamation," his *Richard III*, "whom our playgoers had hoped was shelved forever," was "very shabby," his Romeo was ignored, and *King John*, "seldom performed with success," was "barren of startling effects."[28] In spite of the critics, the American was crowded for his farewell benefit, *Othello*, on July 27. A few days later, McDonough went home to New York. Perhaps sobered by his second encounter with San Francisco, he did not play the West again.

It was almost a year before another star of McDonough's stature came west, and his reception was strikingly similar. James W. Wallack, Jr., came from a theatrical family. Both his father and his grandfather were well known actors, and he had continued in their footsteps. Physically imposing, with a magnificent voice, he was one of the most popular stars on the Eastern stage, and in 1858, Maguire brought him to San Francisco. His appearance was heralded by weeks of publicity, and on March 3 he opened *Macbeth* to a densely packed Opera House.

---

27. Golden Era, *February 15, 1857.*
28. Golden Era, *July 21, 23, 24, 25, 1857.*

The critics were not pleased. Wallack was pronounced, "an actor of considerable genius and power" but "not approaching greatness." His concept of the role was "at best but a faint imitation" of Macready, his "power of expression" was "deficient," and his mannerisms "odious." They especially disliked his studied elocution. "Lay on, Macduff," they said, sounded "very much as a Bowery butcher would in challenging another to fight." Mrs. Wallack, who played Lady Macbeth, came off somewhat better, though the phrases were hardly flattering, "Her masculine voice and strong cast of features peculiarly adapt her for the part."[29]

*Othello* was acceptable, but *Hamlet* was a "rough impersonation," with a "butchered" text. There was the added comment that he lacked Mcready's "electric touch of genius." The harshness was mitigated for *The Iron Mask,* where Wallack was, "in his element — which is not, and never can be, in the more intense and philosophical portraitures of Shakespeare."[30]

The tone began to change with Leontes in *A Winter's Tale,* which was "excellent," with only a touch of sarcasm in the suggestion that he was best in roles requiring no deep philosophy. And Wallack's *Richard III,* a monster of "malignant selfishness . . . canting hypocrisy and cutting satire," won unqualified compliments. It was "most perfect of any actor's now on the American stage," approaching that of Junius Brutus Booth. In this role, his "consummate" acting was "full of expression and originality."[31]

That was the high point. *King John* suffered from long waits and miscues; it was suggested that Wallack (Falconbridge) and June Booth (John) should have switched roles. Mrs. Wallack, whose Gertrude in *Hamlet* and "classic, calm" Hermione in *A Winter's Tale,* had been admired, was also praised for her Constance, but the rest of the cast was below standard and the supers were clumsy. Still, when the Wallacks set off on a mine tour, the papers generously called them, "probably the best delineators of the legitimate drama that have ever been in California."[32]

29. Golden Era, *March 7, 1858.*
30. Golden Era, *March 14, 1858.*
31. Golden Era, *March 28, 1858.*
32. Golden Era, *March 28, 1858.*

Sacramento greeted them more warmly than San Francisco, but accounts differ about their tour of the mines. The papers reported "large houses," but George Ryer, who managed the tour, said they had made "a slim mess of it."[33] That seems more likely, for on their return to San Francisco, a short engagement at the American yielded only small returns. In July 1859, they went home, like many other Eastern stars disillusioned and disinclined to make a second attempt.

During the time the Wallacks were on tour, James Anderson arrived. An Easterner with a good reputation as a tragedian, he first appeared without fanfare touring Grass Valley, Marysville, and Nevada City, where his Hamlet was admired as "so natural ... that one is disposed to imagine it a reality."[34]

By mid–May 1859, he was in Stark's San Francisco company as a star "who comes to us with great reputation,"[35] alternating *Hamlet* and *Othello*, with Stark as Iago. The reviews were encouraging until the Bakers hired him to star with Alexina. Then the critics did an about face and commented acidly that his Romeo was the "most debased and unnatural ever known."[36] Whether it was the biting words or the difficulty of touring and acting on rough-hewn Western stages, Anderson decided that two months was a fair enough trial. *Romeo and Juliet* was his last performance in California.

The Bakers recovered by bringing James K. Hackett to the American in April, 1860. The corpulent actor, called "Baron" because he claimed a titled Irish ancestor, had been a star for nearly forty years. His Falstaff was undoubtedly the greatest of the century, and he revealed its dimensions in *Henry IV, Part 1,* and *The Merry Wives of Windsor.* For those who did not attend the theater, he read these plays, *Hamlet,* and other Shakespearean works for clubs. One of the few Easterners to meet with wholehearted acclaim in California, he found his visit short but very sweet.

Far from sweet was the reaction to Harry Perry at San Fran-

33. *Edmond M. Gagey,* The San Francisco Stage *(New York: Columbia, 1950), p. 82.*

34. Nevada Democrat, *May 5, 1859.*

35. California Spirit of the Times, *May 14, 1859.*

36. California Spirit of the Times, *May 28, 1859.*

cisco in July, 1860. Billed as "the greatest living actor," the Philadelphia-born Perry had begun a promising career with a New York debut in 1847 as Malcolm in *Macbeth*. Handsome, charming, and debonair with exceptional talent both as an actor and mimic, he was also an alcoholic. After several notable seasons in Philadelphia, he was invited to star in New Orleans during the 1851–52 season, an engagement that terminated abruptly when Perry, celebrating a friend's departure for Mobile, forgot to leave the ship when it sailed. Over the next nine years, a string of contracts were broken for the same convivial reason. If Perry could stagger onto the stage, he was brilliant, but by 1860 those days were rare. At the age of thirty-four, he was a physical wreck. He played a splendid Romeo to Julia Dean Hayne's Juliet, but the papers were not kind to his Benedick, Othello, or Shylock, and his season in San Francisco was short.

For some reason, he stayed in California and, in December, 1860, toured with one of the several "Star" companies on the eastern edge of the gold fields. June Booth was also in that company, and they gave a number of Shakespeare plays. Perry seemed to be making an effort to overcome his problem, and in 1861 he married Agnes Land, a young Australian actress, but it was too late. Within a year, he was dead.[37]

Between 1860 and 1865, few stars came west. Many actors were involved in the Civil War, travel was almost impossible, and the prospectors' largesse ceased when mining became an industry. One of those who dared to make the journey was the English actor Charles Dillon. He had been a star at Sadler's Wells for fifteen years when he made his American debut in 1861 at New York's Winter Garden. He might have stayed there longer but for the Civil War, which so unnerved him that he was afraid to remain in such unsettled conditions. Like many before him, he decided to make his fortune in California.

His first appearance in San Francisco started off well. His *Richard III* was so memorable that thirty years later John Q. Adams recalled his "thrilling voice" in the lines,

37. *Agnes Perry married June Booth in 1862, and, after his death, John B. Schoeffel in 1885.*

> I have set my life upon a throw, —
> I will stand the hazard of a die.[38]

He played only three nights, however, before falling so ill that the engagement had to be ended. This was only the first of many difficulties.

When Dillon was well again, he set out for the mines, but in Oroville, he had played only a few days when the rains began. They continued for seventy-seven days and produced the great flood of 1862 which "treed" McKean Buchanan. The Oroville theater was unreachable after first night, the hotel after three days, the town at the end of the week. He fled to Sacramento. There he gave one performance and the next day was rehearsing *Hamlet* when word came that the levees had broken and the town was in danger. In five minutes, the river was rushing into the pit. The company waded through waist-high water to the highest point where they helped construct makeshift rescue rafts. By nightfall, the entire city was three feet below the surface of the waves.

He tried the mountains; in Marysville, he saw a hotel "as large as the Euston-Square hotel" entirely inundated, at Stockton and Grass Valley, not a single structure was left standing. Moving from town to town by boat, he returned to San Francisco and found one third of that city demolished. Since the rest was habitable, he played a week's engagement, earning his passage to Australia with a superb Othello and Lear, only to be struck down again when a broken ankle confined him to bed. On recovery, he learned it would be four months before the next ship sailed.

In desperation, he started for Vancouver by land and reached that city only after being snowbound several weeks on the way. His experiences, which also included a frightening confrontation with Flathead Indians and several ferocious audiences, made him refuse to come west again. When he reached England at last, he stayed there except for a single visit to New York in 1866.

Despite the disasters, Dillon was extravagantly admired and treated as an honored guest wherever he played. In turn, aside

38. Recollections of Early Theatricals in San Francisco, *essay read before the California Historical Society, April 8, 1890, pp. 20–30.*

from his disapproval of their "American manners," he liked the rough, honest miners and was impressed by their generosity. He never forgot that, in spite of their own sufferings after the Oroville debacle, they had arranged a special benefit for him.

The influx of stars slowed to a trickle, and the last one did not appear for two more years. Charles Kean, son of the legendary Edmund Kean, had made his debut at Drury Lane in 1827 at the age of sixteen and was soon a star in his own right. Watching the elder Kean, Coleridge once said, was like reading Shakespeare by flashes of lightning. Watching the son must have been more like reading by a fluorescent lamp. Calm, earnest, with a repose that bordered on immobility, Charles Kean was an actor who studied and practiced his craft diligently, who rehearsed every move, every gesture, every intonation until it was perfect. For Americans, a slight nasality marred his voice, but his diction was clear and precise, and his performances were works of art lacking only one ingredient — inspiration.

After his first visit to America in 1831, he married Ellen Tree, attractive daughter of an acting family. Although she was loftier physically and artistically, she subordinated her career to his. They toured America together in 1847, and if managers tended to hire them because of her gifts, the fact was never mentioned in his presence.

In 1864, as the most famous acting couple in England or America, they played New Orleans, then crossed Panama to visit Australia. On their way home, they stopped in California long enough to give a short season that included *Henry VIII*. San Franciscans considered them "mannered," but were mightily impressed with the polish and quality of their acting. They pleaded for more, although had they known Kean's private opinion of the "snuffling, spitting, chewing Yankees," they might have been less cordial.

The Keans had contracted to play in Vancouver and could not stay long, but before leaving they agreed to return for another engagement. They kept their word and in January 1865 came back to San Francisco for a season that included *Merchant of Venice, Hamlet, Othello, Much Ado about Nothing, King John* and a *Richard III* in which a young and unknown David Belasco played the Duke of York. In all, they gave sixty performances. Kean's prejudice against Americans was not in the least ameliorated by the $30,000 they took home with them.

Stars were important to the Western theater. Their own high professionalism elicited better performances from other actors and raised the level of performance until critical faculties were honed to razor sharpness. From the distance of more than a century, the records of their various appearances indicate a gradual change. As the years passed, local actors developed a different and distinctly Western style. Far from the "rant" and bravura that has sometimes been suggested, it was freer, less schooled, with its own subtleties. After 1855, carefully trained Eastern actors were often reproached as "stiff," "formal," or "mannered" by California critics; conversely, with rare exceptions, Western-bred actors seldom succeeded in New York. Manners and modes had vastly different expressions in the traditional East and the unconventional West, and what seemed perfectly natural on one coast appeared alien to the other.

Nevertheless, most stars conquered such distinctions along with other obstacles like crude stages, mountain storms, and the lack of civilized amenities. Each of the dozen noted here made a special contribution, some by virtue of personality, others by new interpretations, but all producing a high level of drama in the wilderness. Lonely miners who might have been equally satisfied with flea circuses, soon recognized and demanded the best from actors. More often than not, they got it.

# Women and Children First

Female stars occupied a special place in the Gold Rush galaxy and often gleamed with a brighter glow than the men. In the overwhelming male domain of the early West, the very appearance of a woman in a mining camp was greeted with applause. Even the cities were predominantly masculine; in 1850, Captain Coffin, newly arrived in San Francisco, saw "scarcely a bonnet" in church.

Among the women who did come west, health and strength were more important than beauty, and there was no place for the delicate girl who fainted at the slightest provocation, although she remained an ideal. Actresses combined strength with the appearance of delicacy and could give the illusion of beauty even when they were not particularly attractive. It is small wonder that miners grew rhapsodic over them.

In some ways, the life of a touring actress was more difficult than for her male counterpart. True, she did not have to fight bears, but tightly laced corsets and floor-length skirts were not ideal for mountain and desert terrain. Town life offered its own hazards: rough-planked boardwalks were embarrassingly full of long splinters that caught and shredded the dust ruffle on an unwary lady's petticoat. Men could appear bearded and unwashed without reproof, but actresses were expected to be permanently well-groomed and clean, not to say rather elegant. Such matters may seem unimportant in the life-and-death struggle for survival, but to women whose livelihood depended on their appearance, these *were* survival.

They had to be as versatile as the men, and several even played male roles. The most frequent choice was Romeo, which gives an indication of how the nineteenth century viewed the role—not as a hot-blooded young Italian, but as an innocent youth, chaste and romantic. The sexlessness of a female Romeo appears to have been its greatest appeal, and Noah Ludlow went so far as to say the role *required* a boy rather than a man.[1]

Like the men, most of them brought established names from the East. One of the earliest, however, was strictly a Western product who began and ended her career in California. Harriet Carpenter is first mentioned as a member of the Robinson troupe playing Nevada City in June 1851, but a few months later she was a leading woman at the Jenny Lind in San Francisco. Under June Booth's coaching, she was complimented for her "easy, natural, and pleasing" style, as Anne in his *Richard III,* singled out as an actress with "talent and the personal attractions for a wide range of theatrical business" who "cannot fail of becoming one of the first actresses on the Pacific Coast."[2]

She rarely stayed long in any company. In December, 1851, she left Booth to join the Starks at the American, perhaps hoping for a greater range of parts. She got them in Stark's productions: Ophelia in *Hamlet,* Goneril in *King Lear,* and the male role of Malcolm in *Macbeth,* but her gifts were limited. Malcolm was only "passable," and when she tried comedy in *Poor Pillicuddy,* the comment was a succinct, "Kate Gray played the character of Mrs. Pillicuddy very well; Miss Carpenter that of Sarah Blount just the opposite."[3]

For an ambitious young actress, supporting roles were not satisfactory, and after a few weeks, she quit the Starks' company and the San Francisco stage for a time. She probably went back

1. Dramatic Life as I Found It *(St. Louis: G.I. Jones, 1880), p. 316.*
2. Evening Picayune, *October 2, 1851.*
3. Evening Picayune, *December 16, 1851.*

to the more lucrative camp tours, where she had her choice of star-ring roles. Somewhere in her travels, she met and married Ben Moulton, a bluff, hearty stagecoach driver with an eye for pretty women, who immediately retired from driving to manage his bride's career. They toured the mines until 1854 when she arrived in Mokelumne Hill as a "star."

The title was premature. Three years of touring isolated camps meant only experience without improvement. Lonely miners were undiscriminating in their approval of actresses, and Harriet had developed so many mannerisms that she arrived in Mokelumne Hill a stilted, mechanical actress. The extravagant playbills brought full houses for a few days; after that she played to empty seats. Moulton vanished, but Harriet stayed on, collecting the fat salary guaranteed her by an iron-clad contract.

Facing bankruptcy, the management was in despair. Fortunately for them, Harriet had become such a devotee of spiritualism that she insisted on interrupting rehearsals for seances. At one of these sessions, her first question was about her husband — had he gone to San Francisco? The table, well prepared by the managers, tipped once for yes.

"Was there anybody with him?"

"Yes."

"Was it a man?"

The table tipped twice, meaning "No."

"A woman?"

"Yes."

Harriet "rose with blood in her eyes, went straight to the stage office, bought a seat, and the next morning started for San Francisco, breaking her contract to smithereens."[4] The managers were saved.

Apparently she found Moulton and removed him from temptation by taking him to Hawaii where, reportedly, she was a great success. A year later, San Francisco thought she "would be a valuable acquisition to the San Francisco boards."[5] She did not oblige them but chose to tour as the star of her own company.

---

4. *Ayers, p. 138.*
5. Golden Era, *January 7, 1855.*

In July, 1856, after a brief season in Sacramento, Moulton organized the "Star Company" with Edwin Booth as Harriet's leading man. In a large covered wagon decorated with advertisements of their shows and drawn by four fine horses, they set off on a tour extending from Placerville through Georgetown, Angel's Camp, Diamond Springs, Auburn, and Grass Valley to Nevada City. Unfortunately, California was in the midst of the depression, and they reaped more praises than cash. Compounding their distress, a series of fires followed their appearances, with appalling regularity, and although there was clearly no connection between the company and the conflagrations, superstitious miners began to avoid them, and attendance declined even further.

At Downieville, Moulton, as he had done several times before, departed the scene, this time taking the horses and wagon with him. Harriet and her troupe walked to Sacramento. Booth supported her in a benefit that repaired her purse well enough to take her on to San Francisco where, in January, 1857, she divorced Moulton. He was later shot by an irate husband.

She resumed her maiden name and continued acting, but without much success. Harriet Carpenter was not a great actress. With careful management and plays tailored to her limited powers, she might have done fairly well. Indeed, from 1851 to 1855, she was most certainly a star to hundreds of lonely miners, but as the competition grew stronger, she could not hold her place. For a few months after the divorce, she played in small towns, but by the end of the year, her name disappears completely and she is heard of no more.

One of her strongest rivals was another divorcée, Catherine Sinclair, whose sensational court battle with Edwin Forrest was still fresh enough to draw full houses. She came west in 1853 and, although no better an actress than Carpenter, with several advantages. She was exceedingly beautiful, recognized her limitations, and earned considerable respect by her managerial skills.

Her marriage to Forrest must at first have seemed a great match to an eighteen-year-old girl from a middle-class family. The handsome Forrest was rich and famous, the first genuine American-born star, a dazzling performer whose athletic performances brought cheering audiences to their feet.

The differences between them, however, were deep and divisive. Big, bluff Forrest had hearty appetites for eating, drinking and making love. He was also a consummate egoist, insensitive to others, demanding, coarse, uneducated and undisciplined. A product of American Puritanism (his father had been a Scotch Presbyterian), he believed fervently in the double standard and practiced accordingly, although he expected her to be chaste, faithful, and forgiving. Catherine was a cultivated young woman, in appearance demure and unassuming, in manner gentle. As thoroughly English as Forrest was American, her tastes, friends, and style of living differed markedly from his.

During the twelve years of their marriage, Forrest had innumerable affairs, but he was also an inordinately jealous husband. When he discovered an actor in his company had been writing her extravagant love letters, he was so infuriated that he drove her from his house and sued for divorce. She countersued, made much of his extramarital affairs, and in December, 1851, was awarded $3,000 a year alimony.

Forrest refused to pay and appealed the decision, which began a long, slow trek through the courts. In need of money, Catherine turned to the stage. Her debut in February 1852 was a lukewarm success that created as many problems as it solved. She appeared as "Catherine Forrest," outraging many, including her former husband, who felt she was trading on his name. Going back to her maiden name, Sinclair, did not help. The divorce had made her a fallen woman, and many people openly condemned her. Many managers loyal to Forrest and the box office, would not engage her until Tom Maguire, accurately regarding her notoriety as an advantage in California, offered escape from the shadow of scandal, and a chance to make a fortune.

She arrived on May 9, 1853, and June Booth presented her at San Francisco Hall the next day. San Franciscans liked her very much. The reviews praised her grace, her elegance, and her ladylike deportment, and a crowded house saw young Edwin Booth play Benedick to her Beatrice:

> No piece that has been played in our city for a long time has met
> with the singular makers of popular favor as much as *Much Ado*

*about Nothing.* In fact, Beatrice is probably Mrs. Sinclair's best part.[6]

After two weeks, she went to Sacramento for a brief visit, taking Edwin along as her leading man. On their return, she moved over to the American to replace Alexina Baker for the summer, playing Beatrice to Lewis Baker's Benedick and Queen Katharine in his premiere of *Henry VIII.*

In September, marking time until she could take over the management of Maguire's grand new Metropolitan,[7] she gave Shakespearean readings for the Music and Drama Festival and played occasionally for June Booth. When he presented *The Merchant of Venice* with young Edwin Booth as an outstanding Shylock, she was perfectly able to hold her own:

> As Portia, Mrs. Sinclair acquitted herself with much credit, her performances in the court scene being in our opinion, the most judicious and excellent piece of acting she has rendered on the San Francisco boards.[8]

On December 13, with C.F. Thorne as Othello and Edwin as Iago, she played her first Desdemona. She was overshadowed but not condemned.

The Metropolitan opened on December 24, 1853, and Sinclair gave the first indication of her managerial talent by hiring June Booth as stage manager. A week later, they gave *Hamlet* with James Murdoch as the star and Sinclair as Ophelia, followed by an *Othello* in which she played Desdemona to his Moor. Commended for her management, she was less admired for her acting, and the papers complained that Murdoch's appearances were marred by poor support. Sinclair, they wrote,

> *tries* to please, and for which she deserves much credit — but nine times out of ten, her overwrought efforts prove painful . . . and render the whole performance anything but effective.[9]

6. Placer Times, *May 24, 1853.*
7. *First known as the San Francisco, its name was soon changed by Sinclair.*
8. Placer Times, *September 9, 1853.*
9. Golden Era, *January 8, 1854.*

Maguire had no doubt hired her, as he had June Booth, because of her theatrical connections, and she did bring stars to the Metropolitan: opera diva Anna Thillon, the Irish comedian Barney Williams, the Bateman children, and the infant prodigy, Anna Maria Quinn. Not all were people she had known in the East; some were engaged because she had a good eye for talent. She must have seen the unknown Matilda Heron when she first played for the Bakers and, sensing her powers, starred her at the Metropolitan when they went touring. Heron became an immediate and special favorite.

By spring 1854, the papers, forgetting earlier encomia heaped on the Starks and Bakers, eulogized her management: "Mrs. Sinclair has certainly done more towards the permanent establishment of the legitimate drama in California than any other person."[10] She gave a benefit for the Firemen's Charitable Fund and raised $5,000, the largest amount ever collected in one evening, and her complimentary benefit in July played to an overcrowded house.

Yet all was not well. She had brought stars, but she had also paid them generously; it was rumored that some had earned $30,000 or more, and despite box office receipts of $400,000, her first year ended with a deficit. By August, business was so poor that the owners gave her a free week of performance, but they had enough confidence to retain her for another year.

She concentrated on management, sending to New York for stars and presenting them in lavish productions, restricting her own acting to supporting roles. Still, expenses mounted, and in June, after another *Much Ado about Nothing* with Edwin Booth, a farewell benefit marked the end of her career as a San Francisco manager.

Following the standard pattern, she set off for the interior. A prosperous season in Marysville led to a tour of the mines, and she reaped a golden harvest from Downieville, Rough and Ready, Camptonville, Forest City, Grass Valley, and Nevada City. In September 1855, she returned to San Francisco to play Portia for McKean Buchanan before taking over the Sacramento theater and

10. Golden Era, *May 14, 1855.*

premiering one of the most popular plays of the day, *The Marble Heart,* with Edwin Booth as her leading man.

In January, 1856, after giving *Richard III* for his benefit, she took the company on a month's tour of the mines before returning to Sacramento. At this point, her finances were in excellent shape, she had proved herself as actress and manager, and she was ready to move on. In March, 1856, she went to Australia. Word came back that she did not do well there, and she paid a brief visit to England before settling in New York.

Eleven years later, Forrest was finally forced to pay the divorce settlement (by then $64,000, of which $50,000 went to the lawyers) and to continue the annual $3,000 allowance. In 1874, two years after Forrest's death, the executors of his estate ended the whole matter by paying her a lump sum of $95,000, allowing her to live comfortably until her death on June 17, 1891.[11]

Catherine Sinclair was not a passionate woman, and her English upbringing discouraged displays of emotion, serious handicaps to an actress. On the other hand, her sense of theater allowed her to understand the power of emotion even when she could not produce it. Without the slightest hint of jealousy, she presented actors who could electrify an audience, and she was one of the first to recognize this quality in Matilda Heron.

The Irish-born Heron landed in San Francisco on December 23, 1853, under the most adverse circumstances. Her agent's death on the way to California left her without money or friends, and she arrived with no credentials except her own claims. Her very appearance was against her, for she was unfashionably thin and so plain that only her flashing black eyes kept her from outright ugliness. She had, however, diligence and determination. She had studied with the dramatic coach Peter Richings who promoted the "French school" of acting that stressed intensity over broad gesticulation and theatrical elocution, and she managed to convince the Bakers of her talent. They gave her the chance she needed.

On January 2, 1854, they presented *Romeo and Juliet* with Alexina Baker playing Romeo. As always, Alexina was well

11. New York Times, *June 24, 1891.*

received, but Matilda Heron's Juliet stunned the audience and garnered the reviews. No one had seen anything like it:

> The lovesick girl — not yet a woman — was continually crouching on the ground, or fawning on the nurse or her lover — just like a girl, who had not learned the conventional manners of a thorough-bred lady, which might have prompted her to moderate them a little. But "Juliet" was so youthful, and an Italian too, that perhaps Miss Heron's representation of the part was only the more interesting from the excessive warmth and *abandon* with which it was given.[12]

Frederick Ewer, the stern critic of the *Pioneer*, gives an idea of this abandon along with a suggestion of how the potion scene was usually played:

> Most actresses approach as near to ranting in this scene as it is possible. They tear their hair and appear to be actually beating out someone's brains with the bones of their ancestors. But with Miss Heron, how different. Everything was subdued, the more frightful passages were whispered with indescribable terror. The effect was sublime and the audience breathless.[13]

Like most nineteenth-century productions of *Romeo and Juliet*, the final scene of reconciliation between the Montagues and Capulets was cut, and the play ended with the death of Juliet. Ewer's description of Heron's performance is graphic evidence of the effect she produced:

> as she drew herself toward the body of Romeo, she did not (having reached him) drop her head suddenly upon his breast, as though exhausted nature had given way before she could reach the end attained. It dropped slowly down, and having rested there, sweetly she "fell asleep." Though it was in death, she had indeed reached the loved form at last and was happy. All was silent and holy. The instant when her spirit took its flight we did not know. No time

12. MacMinn, *quoting the critic, Soule, p. 104.*
13. Pauline Jacobson, City of the Golden 'Fifties *(Berkeley: University of California, 1941), p. 219.*

was marked by her for the burst of applause. Every eye was upon her, and the audience waited through the time of the last sad breath, while the hush of death itself was upon them. The curtain fell slowly, and they still looked. The effect was temendous, and it was a moment or two before they recovered.[14]

They were most pleased by the lack of "rant" in her performance: "Her most effective strokes are perhaps a simple look, a curl of the lip, a low muttered sentence, or a bare whisper. Much of her acting as 'Juliet' might be called dumb show; yet it was not the least effective on that account."[15]

The Bakers were about to depart on tour, but they stayed in San Francisco long enough to give Heron a benefit on January 15, 1854. At once Catherine Sinclair invited her to the Metropolitan where she starred for a notable twelve consecutive nights with Edwin Booth as her leading man. He played Romeo to her Juliet, and in return she played Ophelia in *Hamlet*.

At the end of February, she set off for the profitable mining camps. She conquered Stockton and Sacramento as easily as San Francisco. Marysville, disappointed at having to wait an extra week when her Sacramento engagement was extended, kept track of her every move. When she finally reached the town, it too joined in the "Heronry." The actress, "who came amongst us so loudly heralded by Fame's trumpet, proved herself to be all that Fame had pictured her."[16] She introduced a "new and popular school in histrionics," following only "the promptings of her own exquisite genius."[17] She sent the editor of the paper a portrait of herself, and he responded with a rhapsodic description of her Juliet:

> In her amorous scenes her eyes seem to float in liquid love — her whole being appears as an angel — she seems as if she were made for love, and were ready to live and die for it. You love her, in spite of all the matrimonial bonds, fastened upon you by laws human or divine, and she holds you in thraldom to the end of the piece. In her scenes of sorrow and grief, she excites the sympathies

14. *Jacobson, p. 220.*
15. *MacMinn, quoting Soule, p. 104.*
16. Marysville Herald, *March 28, 1854.*
17. Marysville Herald, *March 29, 1854.*

of the coldest; and even the dull, sluggish sympathies of the stoic's heart bubbles up with a tear of tribute to her power. In her scenes of hope and fear, of joy and anguish, her soul plays upon her countenance, like lights and shadows upon the rippling stream, or delicious music around the source from which it emanates. But in her scenes of scorn and contempt, you involuntarily shrink back — daggers seem to gleam from her eyes — and withering curses, quivering from her lips, seem about to light upon you, to sink your soul to perdition."[18]

Marysville was reluctant to lose this "paragon of actresses," and she had to play an extra weeek. Her final night was a scene of lamentations and gifts. She responded with a touching speech:

> Three months ago, I reached California, a nameless wanderer; and in that short space of time, she has not only given me what I chiefly came in search of — my health — but she has crowned me with fame, enriched me with dear friends, and given me the foundation of an ample fortune. God bless California![19]

She told them she was leaving for Europe, to study "and perfect myself in my beloved profession." The statement was not entirely true. She and Ned McGowan had leased a theater in Stockton, where they opened two days later. They closed quickly after a bitter quarrel.

Back in San Francisco in May, she again triumphed as Juliet to Susan Denin's Romeo, but when she tried Lady Macbeth, Ewer complained that she had lost her "naturalness," that she strained for effect, and relied on tricks, "tightly shutting her eyes, keeping them closed for eight or ten seconds, and then opening them suddenly to semi-astonish us with their brightness and blackness."[20] Nevertheless, her farewell performance at the Metropolitan on May 29 was a gala evening, and she left considerably richer in name and purse than when she arrived.

She was in California only six months, but on the strength of that experience, she returned to New York as a star, leaving

18. Marysville Herald, *April 7, 1854.*
19. Marysville Herald, *April 9, 1854.*
20. MacMinn, *pp. 101–102.*

behind mixed feelings about her ability. A year later the *Golden Era* cheerfully reported her reputation was "fading" when actually the reverse was true. Her emotional style caught on in the East, and she became one of the most famous Camilles in American history — so identified with the role that "Camille," engraved on a silver plate, was fastened to her coffin.

On a lighter note, Catherine Sinclair also presented novelties like child stars. Children of theatrical families often played small roles in their parents' companies, but child stars were rarities that drew immense audiences. The West, with even fewer children than women, greeted them with adoration. Little Sue Robinson, the "Fairy Star," and the incomparable Lotta Crabtree were living evidence that talented children could produce showers of gold. So many parents tried to profit by their offspring that eventually even the miners tired of them and put up signs with the firm message, "One-horse theaters and infant prodigies are requested to pass this camp."[21]

In 1854, however, even San Francisco had not become so jaded, and gifted children were treated as wonders. The first, and perhaps the most remarkable, was Anna Maria Quinn. Daughter of an Irish actor, she was born on a Mississippi steamboat in 1848 and made her stage debut in St. Louis exactly five years later.

In April, 1853, the parents set out for California, earning their way by driving cattle. It was November before they reached San Francisco, where Mrs. Quinn found work as a costumer for the Thorne company. Soon, Anna Maria was playing Little Eva in their production of *Uncle Tom's Cabin,* and so much of its success was due to her that she was engaged by the Metropolitan. Here she acted Fleance in *Macbeth,* Prince Arthur in *King John,* and Young Norval in *Douglas,* but her greatest moment came on June 21, 1854, when her Hamlet (Act I only) "took the house by storm" with its "almost incredible . . . depth of thought and comprehension." Measured against Master Betty, Clara Fisher, and other juvenile stars, she came off well:

> She is a bright-eyed, beautiful little girl, not yet seven years old.
> In her strut, positions and declamatory portions of the act, she

21. *Golden Era, April 12, 1857.*

succeeded admirably, and with judicious training has a fair prospect of becoming a real phenomena [sic] . . . the very best juvenile
Hamlet we ever saw."[22]

Her achievement was as ephemeral as childhood. In
September, her manager and coach, a Mr. Vinson, took her and,
presumably, her parents to Australia's gold fields. Four years later,
she appeared in New York and, on September 8, 1858, in London,
but never again did she duplicate the remarkable impression she
made on San Francisco.

Sinclair also presented Kate and Ellen Bateman, then nearing
the end of their short but sensational careers as child wonders.
Their parents, Hezekiah Linthicum Bateman, and his wife,
Sidney Cowell, were both players, and the two little girls had been
on the stage since infancy. They were unusually precocious, a fact
quickly appreciated and utilized by their parents. On December
1, 1849, they presented Kate and Ellen, aged six and four respec-
tively, in Shakespearean scenes at the St. Charles Theater in St.
Louis. The girls were an immediate and phenomenal success. Five
years later, they were seasoned veterans with a trunkful of glowing
reviews from American and European critics.

Like London, Paris, New York, and Boston, at first San
Francisco was deeply suspicious of the highly advertised moppets.
They opened on April 15, 1854, and, as in every other city, their
audiences were thrilled by scenes from *Richard III, The Merchant of
Venice, Macbeth,* and *Hamlet.*

Kate, now eleven, was judged more beautiful but less accomplished, and there were some reservations about her "mechanical"
delivery as Richmond in *Richard III* and Portia in *The Merchant of
Venice* but nine-year-old Ellen's Richard and Shylock won
wholehearted acclaim, while her Lady Macbeth was so "fiendish"
that it was suggested she must be a "changeling," who looked like
a little girl "but in thought, facial expression, tones and manner"
was "an old devil incarnate."[23] In her Hamlet, the critic found "in-
tellect, native as well as acquired; intelligence and feeling which

22. Golden Era, *June 28, 1854.*
23. MacMinn, *p. 103, quoting Soule.*

did not come from without, but which flowed outwards from the head and heart, and carried with them the heads and hearts of the audience."[24] The normally cool *Alta California* called her "chaste, touching and impassioned delineation of the broken-hearted prince" masterful:

> Voice, reading, grace of attitude, and nobility of mien and car-riage seemed the genuine inspirations of genuine feeling. The child vanished on assuming, Minerva-like, the panoply of the Jove of Avon, and became a prince, with royal tread and heart; the eye of the beholder, expanding with his thought, saw in her the very stature of manhood, as though, through the misty vista of revived tradition, enkindled fancy invested her youthful form with the proportions of manly reality.[25]

Throughout April, 1854, people flocked to see the miniature geniuses, and they would undoubtedly have departed California with the gold they sought, had the parents been less greedy. Not satisfied with crowded houses every night, they devised a scheme to collect an extra bonanza. At the end of April, following the ex-ample of Edwin Forrest, they offered a prize of $1,000 for the best play written for the girls, adding as a further inducement, that it would be produced in the summer.

The contest generated all the interest they could have hoped. To fill time before announcing the winner and, no doubt, to make a bit of extra profit, the Batemans took the girls on tour. Their fame had preceded them, and as "perfect prodigies of histrionic ex-cellence," they were feted wherever they went.[26] Sacramento gave them "diamond-backed watches with gold chatelaines," Ned Bingham begged them to come to Marysville, the Stockton theater could hardly hold the crowds.

On July 2, 1854, at the Union Theater in San Francisco, they announced the winner of the contest was *The Mother's Trust; or California in 1849*. The author wished to remain anonymous but wanted everyone to know the prize money would be donated to the Orphan Asylum. It was a superb advertising coup, worthy of their

24. *MacMinn, p. 464, quoting Soule.*
25. *MacMinn, p. 464, quoting* Alta California.
26. Marysville Herald, *May 15, 1854.*

friend, P.T. Barnum, and it would have been a splendid finale for their visit — except for one small detail: it was soon learned that the anonymous author was none other than Mrs. Bateman. The newspapers united in their condemnation of the "vile" contest, and when it was subsequently discovered that the play had been plagiarized from Alice B. Neal's *All Is Not Gold That Glitters; or California in 1849,* anger blazed hotly.

Curiosity, if nothing else, filled the Metropolitan on the night the play was given, but it was clear the Batemans had outstayed their welcome. The parents did not push their luck, and they sailed for the East a few days later. The girls retired from acting for a time; Bateman became a manager in New York, then went to England where he made theatrical history by introducing Henry Irving to the British public. Both girls returned to the stage as stars in 1859. Kate married an Englishman in 1866, retired, and spent the rest of her life in England; Ellen, married in 1860, continued to act until 1870. Neither ventured west of New Orleans again.

The Bateman children's chief competition came from Susan and Kate Denin, who opened at the American on April 16, 1854, the same night the Batemans opened at the Metropolitan Theater. Although Susan was nineteen and Kate seventeen, and they had made the difficult transition into adult actresses, they were still accorded the preferential treatment given them as child stars.

Born in Philadelphia, they were aged ten and eight when they first appeared as "Dancing Fairies" in *Pizarro.* Soon they were playing the two little princes in *Richard III* and the two Antipholuses in *Comedy of Errors.* By the time they reached California, they had nine years of trouping behind them, and Susan had been married for a year. Kate was a more recent bride, married the day before they started west.

They spent two weeks in San Francisco, acting in several popular works and at least two Shakespeare plays, *Romeo and Juliet,* with Susan as Romeo and Kate as Juliet, and *Katharine and Petruchio* with Susan as Petruchio, Kate as Katharine. In the end, after constant comparisons with the Batemans, the verdict held that the two sets of sisters were equally excellent. When Susan played Romeo to Matilda Heron's Juliet, however, Heron's dynamic acting left the audience breathless, and poor Susan was pronounced a "rude, unfinished piece of inferior art."[27]

The sisters joined C.F. Thorne's troupe and went on tour. Sacramento and Stockton were much kinder than San Francisco, and Marysville prepared a warm welcome when Ned Bingham announced that, "Aside from the rare attraction of these extraordinary sisters, a very superior stock company and orchestra have been engaged."[28] It was sheer bad luck that the season in Marysville ended abruptly when fire destroyed the theater and a good part of their wardrobe.[29]

After two months in California, they left for happier engagements in the East. Both continued successful careers on the stage. Susan married twice more and ended her career in London; Kate married a second time, toured Australia, and returned to end her days in America.

A much more dazzling actress arrived in the midst of Sinclair's management and just on the heels of Matilda Heron's success. English-born Laura Keene was a striking figure. She had been married, widowed, deserted by a second husband, had worked as a barmaid, had studied with Madame Vestris and had become a well-known actress when the elder Wallack brought her to New York in 1852. Performances in New York and Baltimore added to her fame, and when she appeared in San Francisco on April 6, 1854, audiences expected to see a star.

She certainly fit the description. Tall and slender, she was exceptionally beautiful, with an expressive face set off by brilliant dark eyes and framed with auburn hair. Her voice was clear and musical, her movements graceful, her poses statuesque. She also had the personality of a stereotypical star. Winter called her "self-willed, volatile, capricious, and imperious," all of which described her perfectly if one also includes a personal magnetism that riveted attention on her every gesture. With Edwin Booth as her leading man, she played for almost two weeks to mixed reactions. No one was indifferent, and the *Alta California* summed it up neatly:

27. MacMinn, *p. 104, quoting the* Chronicle.
28. Marysville Herald, *May 22, 1854.*
29. Golden Era, *May 28, 1854.*

Her performances have elicited every variety of remark and opinion and have been the cause of some of the most conflicting and opposite criticisms that we have ever seen bestowed upon an actress. By some, she has been pronounced as exceedingly "natural": by others as entirely "unnatural, forced, artificial and studied." Between these two extremes also, a wide range has been afforded for criticism, and in the papers and out of the papers it has been passed upon her. Although Miss Keene has by no means made a failure, it would be useless to deny that she has not made a "hit."

But Keene felt she had failed. She blamed Edwin Booth, although she fared no better when she played Juliet to Susan Denin's Romeo, when the gentle Soule remarked that she "looked just a little too intellectual" for the character. She gained enough ground with her "natural, everyday" Rosalind in *As You Like It*, however, that when it closed, she was given a "massive and elegant" bracelet.[30]

Her feelings were further salved by co-starring with James Murdoch in a successful engagement at Sacramento and by a profitable tour of the mines that gave her enough confidence to try San Francisco again. As actress-manager, she opened the Union while the papers applauded her morality, "We are happy to indorse [sic] it, as we know that strict care is taken to expurgate from the stage anything which might offend the delicate ear."[31]

This time her reception was warmer, but an accident cut the season short when a chandelier fell on her head and cut her face. For Keene, it was a fortunate fall; while she was recuperating, she talked to the Starks, just returned from Australia. When they described the wealth to be garnered, she was suddenly struck with a desire to travel. She may have had an even more compelling reason—the husband who had deserted her was reported to be somewhere in Australia.

Whatever her reasons, she left for Australia at once, sailing on August 1, 1853. Somewhere between spring and late summer, she must have changed her opinion of Edwin Booth, for she took him with her as leading man.

30. Golden Era, *May 21, 1854.*
31. Pioneer, *June 25, 1854.*

Australia gave her a glittering triumph, but the trip had a somber side. Keene, temperamental even in the best of times, became a termagant under stress, and the discovery that her husband was in an Australian prison did nothing to ease her rages. It was a distinct relief to the company when, having achieved both her aims, she decided on a return to California.

They had planned a few performances in Hawaii, but again her temper flared, and this time she walked out, leaving the company to shift for itself. Booth managed to put together a haphazard *Othello* which was attended by King Kamehameha himself, but by the time it was on the boards, Keene was on the high seas.

In March, 1854, she took over the management of the American and began a series of Shakespeare plays. A burlesque *Antony and Cleopatra* erased the over-intellectual image she had created earlier, while her Beatrice in *Much Ado about Nothing* was considered a "fine conception" and an "exquisite interpretation."[32] Like her mentor, Madame Vestris, she surrounded herself with a good company and personally supervised every part of the productions.

The results impressed even the jaded San Franciscans. *Henry VIII,* a reprise of *As You Like It,* and the California premiere of *Twelfth Night* were joyously applauded, although the *Golden Era* said her Viola lacked "pathos and impressiveness," and her acting needed "more passion and greater intensity." *Comedy of Errors,* with Keene as Adriana, was a hit, and her second premiere, *Midsummer Night's Dream,* was the highlight of the season. She was obviously familiar with Madame Vestris' famous London production of the play, for, like Vestris, she chose to play Oberon, and the staging was as near a reproduction as she could engineer. The audience was enchanted:

> The rising moon, the flowing water, which seemed to stretch far back among and under the trees, the flowers opening upon the stage to let Puck out, and to display the fairies, the green banks, woodland glade, sprites — all were admirable.[33]

32. Golden Era, *July 16, 1855.*
33. Pioneer, *June 12, 1855.*

The *Pyramus and Thisbe* interlude was commended, but the greatest charm of all were the small children "but four or five years old apiece," who played the fairies.

Her third premiere, *The Tempest,* was, said the *Golden Era,* "the only stirring event of the week," but tempered its praise. They liked the production, with Purcell's music and a full ballet in the fourth act, but for some reason they did not like the play which they called Shakespeare's "worst."

This was the end of Laura Keene's Western venture. In September, she took her repertory to Sacramento, but the houses were poor, and after a short tour of the mines she went back to her home in the East. She remained in the United States and brought up her two children here. Later, she brought over Madame Vestris and, in her declining years, cared for her in her own home.

To California, she had brought glamour and some excellent productions of Shakespeare. With a fine sense of theater, she surrounded herself with good companies, though she never forgot she was the star. No one was allowed close to the throne; Joseph Jefferson had to leave her troupe in order to make his way to the top. She is probably best remembered, however, for her moment in history, playing *Our American Cousin* for President Lincoln the night he was shot by Edwin Booth's brother.

While Laura Keene was in Australia, two young comediennes captured the California audience. The Gougenheim sisters had been stars in New York since their debut in 1850. Five years later, they arrived in San Francisco and within a week the city was at their feet. The rest of the state soon followed when they went on tour. Adelaide was admired for her romantic heroines and for her sprightly humor. They played mostly light comedy and musical shows, but a sparkling *Much Ado about Nothing* made Joey a favorite Beatrice.

After a year of conquests, they went to Australia and repeated their success, returning briefly in 1858 when they concluded another spell of enchantment with *The Merry Wives of Windsor* with Adelaide as Mistress Ford and Joey as Mistress Page. The applause was louder and longer than ever. They spent some time in the East, a season in London, and paid a final visit to California in 1861. Their charm undiminished by marriage, they repeated favorite plays, adding, for good measure, a production of *As You Like It* that sent critics into ecstasies. Joey's Rosalind, they proclaimed, surpassed that of any other actress. Adelaide then retired to London with her husband, Joey to Australia with hers. Neither appeared again in the West, but their names and their three ventures into Shakespeare were long remembered.

Of those who came with established reputations, the most prominent was Jean Margaret Davenport. Born in London in 1829, she was the daughter of a theatrical manager, the original, it was said, of Dickens' immortal Vincent Crummles in *Nicholas Nickleby*. Unlike Crummles, the real life Davenport was no mere exploiter of a talented child, and although at the age of five Jean was already starring as Richard III and Shylock, he saw to it that her stage training was thorough and rigorous. When she was nine and a veteran of several European tours, he took her on an American tour from New York to New Orleans. Like other child prodigies, her ability to project character amazed and awed audiences; in St. Louis in 1841, her Richard III was "classically true to nature," her elocution "pure and elegant," her acting free of false effects.[34] Davenport's care of his daughter's training proved valuable when, in October, 1850, she made her debut as an adult actress in *Adrienne Lecouvreur*. The promise of the child was fulfilled in the woman, and she became at once a star of considerable magnitude.

Like other major stars, she was lured west by the tales of fortune. She came to San Francisco in March, 1855, preceded by a massive publicity campaign. Still in her mid-twenties, petite, attractive, with two decades of experience behind her, she might have expected the same warm response she had met in other cities. Not so. The heavy promotion proved a disadvantage when her first appearances met with the cool observation that she had been over-advertised and "failed to meet the expectations." Her Pauline in *Lady of Lyons* was all right, though it lacked warmth and tenderness, but as Parthenia in *Ingomar the Barbaian,* the critics found her voice "wanting in modulation and inexpressive of

34. *William G.G. Carson,* Managers in Distress: The St. Louis Stage, 1840–1844. *(St. Louis Historical Documents Foundation, 1949) p. 125.*

delicate pathos or deep feeling." Her Juliet seemed mechanical, betraying "a very early apprenticeship to the profession," and they complained that, "The actress is always present, but the soul that should inspire every motion and utterance does not gleam forth."[35]

These were the comments of critics loyal to their own favorites. The audience may have considered her studied, but they liked her, and her adaptation of the shocking new French play *Camille,* with Edwin Booth as Armand, drew full houses. She had not come to play only San Francisco, however, and in April she left to seek the legendary gold of the interior.

Sacramento and Stockton were no different from San Francisco, and the tour was so unprofitable that by the time she reached Marysville she demanded half the house receipts. That news enhanced neither her reputation nor the box office, and after a final engagement at the Metropolitan, she sailed for the East.

Five years later, a return visit met with exactly the opposite response. In July, 1860, she began a tour in Sacramento that stretched as far east as Salt Lake City. She chose the best actors she could find to support her in the emotional roles she did best and played to crowded houses everywhere. When she went back east again, she married General Lander and retired from the stage. He was killed in the Civil War in 1862, and, as "Mrs. General Lander," she resumed her stage career until her retirement in 1870.

A less touted but more popular actress was Estelle McCormack Potter. Another Philadelphian who chose the stage, she began acting in Natchez in 1842 and played mostly in the South. Although her New York debut as Juliet was favorably received, she was best known as a leading lady in Memphis, St. Louis, and New Orleans. Perhaps this was because she had married the peripatetic John S. Potter, the manager who opened more theaters than anyone before or since. Potter was a fast-talking, fast-dealing promoter with an astonishing capacity to persuade actors, even stars, to join his companies though he paid them poorly, if at all. When a town had no theater, he built one on credit and moved on before the bills could be collected. His life was a constant migration, and scarcely a city, a town, or a village from Maine to Louisiana

---

35. Golden Era, *March 18, 1855.*

had not received at least one visit from him. A dreamer constantly in search of fresh fields, the El Dorado of the West was an irresistible magnet, and when Catherine Sinclair invited Estelle to San Francisco, he saw the opportunity of a lifetime. They arrived together in March, 1855.

Estelle opened at the Metropolitan on April 1, 1855. She was an attractive leading lady with a good figure, a melodious voice, and an ample repertory, "altogether an agreeable actress." She was not, however, a star like Laura Keene or even Jean Davenport, and although audiences liked her "truthfulness and simplicity," they judged her good but not superior.[36]

John stayed in San Francisco barely long enough to read the reviews. Almost at once he set out to continue his theatrical promotion on a road that would eventually lead as far north as Victoria, B.C., and eastward through Idaho to Salt Lake City. Estelle was no docile wife to follow wherever her husband led. She went to Sacramento and joined a company starring Neafie and Harriet Carpenter.

Here, the houses were good, the praises warm, and she stayed with the troupe when it went to Marysville on the first leg of a tour. More accustomed to rude conditions than most, she had no difficulty moving from place to place, and was soon a favorite from Marysville to Nevada City as "the most natural and graceful actress on the California boards," who gave "general satisfaction in every place she has appeared."[37]

When the tour ended, she established her own company, and while her husband pursued his will-o'-the-wisp career across the Western states, she went her own way as an actress-manager. Her company played both popular centers like Columbia, Sonora, Grass Valley, and Oroville and smaller settlements like Shasta and Yreka. Sometimes she spent a month or more in one place, managing the town's theater, and for some time she co-managed with George Ryer in Weaverville.

In November, 1857, she divorced Potter. Soon after, she married a Mr. McDonald and retired from acting. She wrote, anony-

36. Golden Era, *April 1, 1855.*
37. Golden Era, *May 20, 1855.*

mously, "Passages in the Life of an Actress" and other articles for the *Trinity Journal,* but her heart was in the theater, and two years later, she organized a company to tour the northern mines. In December, 1860, she returned to San Francisco to play one last time at the Wells Opera House, but aside from that one visit, she spent the rest of her life acting and managing small California theaters until her retirement. She was not a major star, but her careful choice of actors and plays and the quality of her productions brought distinguished theater to the small towns and camps across California.

Perhaps the most sincerely worshipped goddess of the stage was Julia Dean. Gentle and lady-like off the stage as well as on, she was tall, willowy, and graceful. Her golden brown hair framed an exquisite face with the complexion of a lily, while an almost indiscernible trace of melancholy added a mysterious charm. As an actress, her credentials were impeccable. Her maternal grandfather, Samuel Drake, was the patriarch of the famous theatrical family allied to the Chapmans, her father was Edward Dean, the actor.

After her mother's premature death, she spent her childhood with the Drakes, but when her father remarried, he reclaimed her. Discovering her talent, he quickly began to capitalize on it, and when she was fifteen, he presented her in New York. She made a substantial name as Julia in *The Hunchback* and three years later was an acknowledged star, admired equally for her beauty and her versatility. Popular everywhere, she was a particular favorite in the South, and her appearances in Charleston, Memphis, St. Louis, and New Orleans invariably drew large and enthusiastic crowds.

In 1855, she married Dr. Arthur Hayne in Charleston and from that time on, billed herself as Julia Dean Hayne. After one more southern tour, they sailed from New York to California, reaching it in June, 1856. Perhaps she had heard of the antagonism met by Jean Margaret Davenport, for she did not begin acting until November, and then in Sacramento instead of San Francisco. She need not have worried. Audiences were delighted with her and preferred her Juliet above that of Catherine Sinclair:

> Her correct style cannot be doubted. Her acting is natural, and her speech is governed by art following nature. The character was

admirably sustained, and the entire play was produced in a manner rarely observed upon a California stage."[38]

As a token of Sacramento's esteem, she was given a diamond brooch when the season ended.

Before bearding the San Francisco lions, she spent the winter touring the mines. Not only settled communities like Stockton, Marysville, and Placerville, but the tiny villages of Coloma, Oroville, Red Bluff, Georgetown and Dutch Flat came to know and love her. By the end of the tour, her reputation was well established, and on her return to Sacramento in February, the reviewer was hard put to find new compliments for her Juliet:

> it would be scarcely possible to speak in terms of too great praise. The whole character was elegantly rendered but some of the best parts were absolute gems, faultless in every particular.[39]

In March, 1857, she conquered San Francisco, where she was pronounced "brilliant." For thirty straight nights the Metropolitan was crowded, and when she moved to the American, the audience followed her.

Popular acclaim in the cities was sweet, but the mines offered just as much, along with even greater financial reward. In May, she set out again and found her reception even warmer than the first time. In Nevada City, *Romeo and Juliet* and *As You Like It* drew the largest audiences ever seen there, and Walter Leman, who was in her company, said they never made less than three hundred dollars a night even in the smallest towns.

On her return to San Francisco in the summer of 1857, she played a series of Shakespeare plays with John Edwin McDonough as her leading man. It was not a good season. Although Hayne's personal appeal had not diminished, San Francisco was in the midst of a depression, banks were failing, and houses were poor. Moreover, the critics were not pleased with McDonough, and were harsh on his Wolsey in *Henry VIII*. The rest of the cast fared no better, except for Hayne's Queen Katharine, which:

38. Daily Town Talk, *November 16, 1856.*
39. Sacramento Union, *February 14, 1857.*

never appeared to finer advantage. She has evidently bestowed upon the play severe study, and her rendition of her part was characterized by an appropriateness of the times, as well as the peculiar character of the injured queen whom she impersonates.[40]

*Richard III,* which they "had hoped was shelved forever," had a slim audience. McDonough, the critic said, was a "very shabby" Richard, and even Hayne was "weak."[41] She was grudgingly admitted to be a fair Constance in *King John,* but the play was "barren of startling effects,"[42] while *Romeo and Juliet* was completely ignored. Audiences rallied enough to give McDonough a full house for his farewell benefit, *Othello,* but as a whole, the summer was a dreary one.

There was nothing for it but to go back to touring, and in October, Hayne gathered her troupe and set off. The first stop was Sacramento, where she received the warmest of receptions. The manager was not happy about her "grand complimentary benefit," but he had to admit that her appearance had markedly improved his box office.

Placerville also gave her a complimentary benefit, and they trouped on to Downieville, to Nevada City, to all the small towns that knew and loved her. Even with full houses and adoring audiences, however, touring was not easy, especially in winter. Not only were the roads and trails choked with snow, accommodations rudimentary, but few theaters had adequate stages. Sheets and blankets were standard scenery, candles and oil lamps still the only lighting, furniture whatever could be begged or borrowed.

Marysville had no balcony for *Romeo and Juliet.* A chair was not high enough to be effective, but the resourceful actors found two empty barrels would do nicely, if a plank were placed over the open tops. Such an expedient did not bother an intrepid adventurer like Hayne, and she gamely climbed up to begin the balcony scene. In the passion of the moment, she must have forgotten where she was, for on the line,

40. Alta California, *July 21, 1857.*
41. Golden Era, *July 23, 1857.*
42. Golden Era, *July 25, 1857.*

> The orchard walls are high and hard to climb,
> And the place death....

she stepped backwards, disappeared into the barrel, and had to be lifted out by Romeo before they could continue — which they did on the solidity of the stage floor.

At the end of that engagement, she announced she was leaving for the Atlantic states, but she did not actually leave until she had played a month in Sacramento and another in San Francisco. After a farewell performance in January, 1858, she sailed for the East. In thirteen months, she had earned $20,000, mostly in the mining camps, mostly in gold.

In October, 1860, she made a second visit to San Francisco, playing at Maguire's Opera House, again to universal admiration. In *Much Ado about Nothing,* her Beatrice was "elegant, lady-like, and graceful, never over-strained, never lacking in the spirit of dignity,"[43] her Juliet combined "that very youthful appearance, manner, and expression, and the full maturity of histrionic powers which are essential...."[44]

At the end of the season, Hayne gathered a company and set off on tour. She found the country much changed; easy gold was gone and with it the wildcat prospectors. Mining had become big business, and working miners were careful of their wages. The fever had not disappeared entirely but the prospectors had moved to Nevada's silver mines. The troupe went east to Silver City, Carson City, Washoe City, and Virginia City which condemned the company but gave Julia a silver bar pin. She was as popular as ever, especially in Salt Lake City, where she was a particular favorite of the Mormons. Brigham Young had a sleigh made for her to use whenever she visited them; when she was absent, it was reserved for honored guests.

In 1864, Hayne returned to Salt Lake City to co-manage their theater with Annette Ince. Two leading ladies with almost identical repertories are not usually friends, but in spite of newspaper attempts to make them rivals, they liked and respected each other.

43. Alta California, *October 9, 1860.*
44. Golden Era, *October 21, 1860.*

Most of their productions were well received except for *Romeo and Juliet* in which Hayne played Romeo to Ince's Juliet. Ince came off well; Hayne, for the first time, met with a faint note of disapproval:

> Mrs. Hayne's make-up as Romeo would scarcely have led even the most imaginative to believe that she was a son of the house of Montague. Though they might have accepted her as a daughter — the woman being too apparent. Aside, however, from the rather incongruous spectacle of two women making love to each other, and shuffling off their respective coils, because there were obstacles to their union, the play went off very well — Mrs. Hayne's reading being excellent.[45]

She remained in the West for another two years, making her home in San Francisco, although she spent most of the time touring. There may have been personal as well as professional reasons for her constant travel, for in September, 1866, she divorced Arthur Hayne for non-support. The circumstances were so much in her favor that even Salt Lake City did not hold it against her and begged her to act there as often as possible. She could not oblige them. After the divorce, she returned east to marry James Cooper. In March, 1868, at the age of thirty-eight, she died in childbirth.

Julia Dean Hayne was neither temperamental nor highly competitive. Gentle in manner, generous both personally and professionally, she was loved by everyone, even other actresses — except for Mary Provost. In 1850, Provost made her debut in Boston at the age of fifteen and from that time on was a leading lady. A very attractive young woman, she loved fine clothes, dressed in the height of fashion, and considered herself a star. She regarded Julia Dean Hayne as her only real rival and played the same repertory in an effort to outshine her. The rivalry was on her part only, for Hayne never showed the slightest jealousy of others. Possibly Provost sensed she was less gifted, a sentiment in which New York, St. Louis, and New Orleans concurred, for she never achieved either the same eminence or affection.

When Hayne came to California, Provost followed. Unlike

45. The Californian, *June 18, 1864.*

Hayne, however, she attacked San Francisco immediately. On January 3, 1857, while Hayne was still out on her first tour, Mary Provost played Beatrice in *Much Ado about Nothing,* one of Hayne's best roles. San Franciscans judged her according to the standards set by Sarah Stark, Catherine Sinclair, and Laura Keene, as well as Julia Dean Hayne, and their verdict was not favorable:

> In all our theatrical experience, and we have been "playing audience" for a number of years, we have never witnessed (McDermott's *Richard III* not excepted) a more harrowing performance than Mrs. Provost's "Beatrice," in *Much Ado about Nothing* on Friday evening last. Having a totally wrong conception of the part, and being at a loss half the time for the words of the text, she mutilated poor Beatrice in the worst manner conceivable.... About the only "point" made in the play was a single *lapsus-tonguae* by Benedict (Mr. J.B. Booth) who, instead of saying "John the Bastard," brought down the house with "John the Baptist."[46]

Hayne's triumphal season at the Metropolitan a few weeks later completed her discomfiture.

Prudently, Provost went on tour with Fleming, her leading man. They avoided Hayne's itinerary, starting at Jackson, and ending at Marysville, where they finished their season early in March. Audiences were poor; when Samuel Colville offered to organize a company and play the larger mining towns, she gratefully turned the management over to him. Under his aegis, they played Folsom's "neat little theater," Stockton, Valleau's theater in Sonora, a week in Columbia, two nights in Chinese Camp, and the entire range of the southern mines. It was one of the few completely unsuccessful tours. The papers ignored her performances and remarked only that she was "beautifully gowned." Even Sacramento was cold — but then, Sacramento had long since fallen in love with Julia Dean Hayne.

In seven months, Provost had had enough. After a farewell benefit at the Metropolitan on July 31, she announced she was leaving for Australia. At least Hayne had never played *there.* The southern continent was much kinder, and Provost stayed there

46. Golden Era, *January 4, 1857.*

three years. Eventually, she went on to London before returning to New York. She visited London a second time in 1868, married an Englishman, and never came home — or to California — again.

An actress with considerably more claims to be Julia Dean Hayne's rival but who refused to compete was Annette Ince. Daughter of a Baltimore theater manager, she began her theatrical career as a dancer in 1849 but turned to acting four years later. Her beauty and talent soon brought her stardom and comparison with Hayne, who was also popular in Baltimore. The rivalry, however, came from those who preferred one over the other, not from the women, who were friends.

Ince came to California with her sister, Caroline, a few months after Mary Provost's ignominious rout. She had been invited to act at the Metropolitan, where she opened May 3, 1857, with a short season of her best plays. At first San Francisco was gently critical; they liked her Juliet and gallantly blamed any shortcomings on a poor supporting cast, but in general they judged her a fair but not "finished" artist. They were won over by her Beatrice and Rosalind and gave her their approval.

At the end of May, she tried Sacramento and Nevada City. Like many other performers, she found a warmer reception than in San Francisco, and her houses were crowded with eager audiences. A brief, unprofitable return to the Metropolitan was followed by a summer tour of the mines under the management of George Ryer. This time, she traveled more. In July, the company played Stockton; in August, a long engagement at Valleau's theater in Sonora ended with an extravagant complimentary benefit; Chinese Camp raved about her.

In September, Bingham engaged her for a week in Marysville. The town liked her, liked the company, and when she played a benefit for Bingham, she raised a "handsome sum." She had been a special favorite in Stockton, and in September they invited her back to open a new theater. In spite of competition with the Pioneer Circus and the San Francisco Minstrels, the theater was filled every night, and they were held over until mid-October. At the closing performance, she was given a bouquet and a richly bound book as a token of citizens' appreciation. She had, they said, raised the "moral purity" of the drama so that women might attend the theater without fear of contamination.[47]

Julia Dean Hayne was also a familiar face in these areas, and once again audiences began to take sides. One critic compared both and came down for Ince, concluding that Hayne's acting was "art," Ince's "nature,"[48] but audiences apparently saw no difference. Oroville asked her to dedicate its new theater, and she obliged before a "large and brilliant audience."[49]

It was something of a letdown, then, to return to a cool San Francisco reception in December, and she didn't stay long. In January, 1858, she sailed for Australia. When she returned in October, she began touring immediately. The miners welcomed her back, and even when they didn't like her in the melodramatic *Fazio,* their criticism was a mild, "her proper character is Cordelia in *Lear.*"[50]

She remained in the West another year, for the most part playing the camps and small towns. Only once did she come to San Francisco; on Shakespeare's birthday, April 23, 1859, she played the Bard himself in *The Golden Age; or, The Poet's Vision.* It was a momentary appearance between tours. The next year, after the season of co-management with Julia Dean Hayne in Salt Lake City, she went back east and, except for a brief visit in 1863, when she played in Virginia City, finished her career there.

The most colorful of the actresses was the handsome Matilda C. Wood, an English comedienne whom Maguire imported for his Opera House "at great expense." Her first appearance on January 24, 1858, was a triumph for her special brand of comedy enriched with music and dance — a forerunner of the English pantomime in which the principal boy is played by a girl. Mrs. Wood was particularly fetching in tights, and her burlesque Shylock in *The Merchant of Venice Preserved* delighted audiences.

She stayed in San Francisco only a few weeks, leaving for Sacramento when the Wallacks arrived. Sacramento's reaction duplicated San Francisco's, and a two-month tour of the mines

47. *MacMinn, p. 105.*
48. Golden Era, *October 4, 1857.*
49. Golden Era, *October 25, 1857.*
50. San Andreas Independent, *October 25, 1858.*

resembled a royal progress. When she returned to San Francisco, the fortune she had earned was further increased by another burlesque, *La Tempesta; or, The Enchanted Isle,* in which she appeared as Ferdinand.

The luster of success was somewhat dimmed by personal problems, and at the end of the year she obtained a divorce from Mr. Wood. Ordinarily divorce meant ostracism, but San Francisco worshipped at her shrine and regarded Mr. Wood as a mere hanger-on. She received the sympathy, the gifts, and an immense audience for her last performance, *Dick Whittington and his Cat,* before she left for England. There too fortune smiled on her, and after her retirement as an actress in 1866, she managed London's St. James Theater for many years.

Two women who starred in brief but noteworthy appearances were Adelaide Neilson and Charlotte Crampton. Neilson came first in March, 1864, at the height of her powers and fame. She arrived with all the accoutrements of the great actress, and the California Theater was filled throughout her entire engagement. San Francisco fell in love with her beauty, her costumes, and the "thrilling accents" of her "silvery tongue:"

> She was superior as Rosalind in *As You Like It* . . . her very presence gave lustre and success to the piece; her winning smile and great sparkling eyes were magical in effect, while in heavy tragedy she rose to loftiest heights of fervid eloquence, as illustrated in her masterpiece, the character of Juliet, wherein every gesture, glance and word seemed but the natural expression of great genius.[51]

At the opposite pole, the erratic Charlotte Crampton arrived without the slightest warning. Crampton, who began as a singer but turned to acting after losing her voice, had been Macready's leading lady, a celebrated figure on Broadway, and a favorite with companies across the country before dropping out of sight about 1860. In December, 1864, she suddenly materialized in Maguire's Opera House and was hired the moment the manager learned her

51. *Adams, pp. 47-48.*

name. Costumes had to be provided, for she had absolutely nothing but the plain brown dress she was wearing, and on December 28, she electrified the audience as Hamlet. Leman says that "rarely had a more philosophical Shakespearean Prince of Denmark been seen."[52] Two days later she vanished as mysteriously as she had appeared.

Primarily because a star's repertory was shaped by the major roles available, women did not bring as much Shakespeare to the West. Men made their reputations in the tragic heroes, but comparable heroines were rare until actresses entered the English theater in 1660. Nineteenth-century actresses played Shakespeare, of course, and most stars acted Juliet, but their best roles were in his comedies: Rosalind, Beatrice, Viola, and Portia. Their tragic powers had to be exhibited in roles stressing pathos not power, like Bulwer-Lytton's *Lady of Lyons* and Dumas' *Camille.*

Women were an important element in Western Shakespearean production, especially during the early fifties. Laura Keene, Julia Dean Hayne, and Annette Ince were major stars whose rich interpretations brought an aura of glamour and sophistication; Catherine Sinclair, Estelle Potter, and many others produced a wide variety of Shakespeare's works that did not always feature their own talents. All of them took companies to the wilderness, to people who would otherwise never have had a chance to see fine drama. But their greatest contribution was, perhaps, in their appeal as women, an appeal that remained long in memory and that associated the name of Shakespeare with a very special pleasure.

52. *Leman, p. 328.*

# The Journeymen

If the Shakespeare invasion can be compared to an army, the amateur players were the civilian scouts on independent forays, while the main troops were the professionals, mostly foot soldiers, whose officers were the stars. There the parallel stops, for theater was not an organized campaign but only a part of that turbulent, massive river that swept thousands to the California shores.

For the most part, actors did not come in organized companies but singly or with a few friends. The lucky ones arrived with contracts in hand, the rest came on speculation. They discovered conditions were quite different from those in the East with its relatively stable theaters. Although there, on the average, players changed companies every three or four years, many chose to spend their entire careers in one town, becoming respected members of the community. No such stability existed in the West where actors were journeymen in more than one sense, almost constantly on the move. In the cities, a "season" often lasted no more than three weeks, tours might hold a company together for a month or more, but never more than a few days in one place. Not surprisingly, many found such insecurity uncomfortable and stayed only a short time, soon returning to the more traditional theaters they knew.

These journeymen were more likely to be types, less versatile, less magnetic than the stars, but good craftsmen who provided able support and often had their own devoted followings. Among theater people, they were almost in as great a demand as the stars, although they did not command high salaries and were never regarded as indispensable. It was not an easy life. Their incomes were small and insecure, without retirement benefits, and if the box office suffered, they did too. They were at the mercy of unscrupulous managers, temperamental stars, the politics of the time, and the uncertain elements, yet they performed nightly whether or not they had eaten dinner, and they smiled gallantly when they marched into a town looking as prosperous as circumstances would allow.

Besides the star, a company consisted of roughly ten people: a leading man and woman, a juvenile and ingenue, a character man and woman, one or two comics, and one or two utility people. Major companies usually collected their companies and performed first in San Francisco, starting their tours from Sacramento. Led by stars like the Starks, the Bakers, James Murdoch, and Julia Dean Hayne, their travels are fairly well documented. Minor companies generally toured and played in cities only occasionally; their leaders are less well known, but during the Gold Rush years, J.A. Neafie, Estelle Potter, and C.F. Thorne were familiar to everyone in the small theatrical world of California.

So many came that it is impossible to list them all, while their extreme mobility makes it difficult even to sketch their careers. Popular as they were in their own time and place, most of the players' names are now lost in history. They were not important enough for biographers or even newspaper obituaries, and only scattered citations in old newspapers or actors' memoirs record their presence on the Western stage. Yet some attention should be paid to the actors and actresses who provided the foundation and chief support of the theater. They may not have been remembered, but without them the theater and its stars would not have been able to function. More to the purpose here — without them, Shakespeare could not have conquered the West.

## Leading Men and Women

Leading men and women often began as juveniles or ingenues and grew into leading roles. A few graduated into the celestial kingdom of stardom, but the majority remained in the ranks, although more often than not they became actor-managers, heading their own companies. Both men and women acted major roles when no star was available but were ready to step aside and provide the main support when one appeared. In this respect, leading women had a slight advantage, for they were more likely to play opposite a visiting star, since female stars usually traveled with their own leading men. Maturity, however, ended the advantage; a leading man could play lovers well into his fifties, but a leading woman was not accepted as a romantic heroine much past the age of forty. Leading players of both sexes generally stayed true to type to the end of their careers. The transition to character roles was an extremely uncomfortable demotion in importance, and psychologically so difficult that most chose to retire rather than attempt it.

John B. Atwater was the leading man and manager of the first professional troupe in California. It was what the nineteenth century called a "snap company," a casual group of professional actors supplemented by amateurs. They made their debut in Sacramento at the Eagle Theater on October 18, 1849, playing melodramas and farces with considerable success until the winter floods washed away the Eagle and most of the city. The actors seized their costumes and caught the first boat to San Francisco where they performed at Washington Hall, an impressive name for the back room of Thomas Maguire's bar. In spite of a minuscule stage and the dim lighting of kerosene lamps, they did extremely well for three weeks, only to discover their treasurer had lost all their receipts playing monte.

The company disbanded, and Atwater joined up with Joseph Rowe as co-manager of the Olympic Amphitheater. His repertory seldom included Shakespeare except when Sarah Kirby was in his company, but his brief season at the Olympic did offer a single performance of *Richard III*. In the spring of 1850, Sacramento's new Tehama Theater was completed, and he returned there until

July, when poor health forced him to give the management to Sarah Kirby and return East.[1]

Atwater was a typical manager and, except for being the first, is not remarkable. In his company, however, were several actors who went on to play in several important Shakespearean productions. Among these was his young leading man, Henry F. ("Hank") Daly, who came around the Horn in 1849. He acted in the Eagle company both in Sacramento and in San Francisco, and in the Tehama company. After Atwater's departure, he joined June Booth at the Jenny Lind and won high praise as a "manly and courtly" Buckingham in *Richard III*, a "chaste and correct" Macduff in *Macbeth*, an actor who had "more of nature than display" in his interpretations.[2]

In December, 1851, he left the Jenny Lind to enter James Stark's company at the Adelphi where he was twice singled out for excellence in *Hamlet*, once for Laertes and once for Horatio, and again for his Cassio in *Othello*. In March, 1852, he was in the Bakers' production of *As You Like It* and that summer rejoined the Jenny Lind company when Junius Brutus Booth came out. He never became more than a supporting player, but by 1853, when he left for the East, he was considered "one of the very best actors in California."[3]

The Australian actor, Nesbit McCron, who brought the ill-fated Hambletons to San Francisco played an unmemorable *Richard III* and *Othello* at Rowe's Circus in 1850. He was in California only a few weeks, but, like Atwater, he presented several actors who became prominent in California, the most notable of whom was Sarah Kirby (later Stark).

One of the most experienced and successful actor-managers was C.F. Thorne, who came West with a reputation firmly established in New York and New Orleans long before he arrived. A handsome man with a fine baritone voice, he was at his best in emotional roles and was particularly admired for his sophisticated

---

1.  *He did not come back to California. After some time as actor and co-manager with his brother-in-law, Langrishe, in Denver, he went further east to establish the first theater in Madison, Wisconsin.*

2.  Evening Picayune, *October 9 and 13, 1851.*

3.  Golden Era, *December 19, 1853.*

villains. In July, 1851, his initial reception at Sacramento was cool, but the less critical camps welcomed him and gave him a profitable tour. Later that year, he went to San Francisco to co-manage a short season with the Starks and, in March, 1852, to play in *As You Like It* for the Bakers.

He was happiest leading his own company, however, and soon went back to touring. In the early months, when entertainment was scarce, he did very well, but he was not a great actor and his range was limited. As the competition increased, audiences grew thinner and more critical until, in January, 1854, he not only faced nearly empty houses in Marysville but severe castigation of his *Richard III:*

> On Tuesday evening, the tragedy of "Richard the Third" (alas, poor William Shakespeare! to what a base use has your greatest creation come!) was produced to a slim audience. To "a man up a tree," the performance might have appeared all right, but many who had seen *the* "Richard," as performed by the elder Booth and Charles Kean, were not altogether satisfied as to *whose* "Richard" it was, whether Shakespeare's, or whether it was "got up" expressly for *that* occasion by some aspiring "supe." According to William Shakespeare's version, but *one* of the great contending armies is vanquished, while in the "Richard" of Tuesday evening, an indiscriminate slaughtering took place, in which "all hands and the cook to boot," were murdered outright — *nary* a one left to tell the piteous tale. During the performance, a wag at our elbow suggested that Richard "was *not* himself" — but some body else.[4]

It was time to leave, and in July, 1854, he sailed for Australia. He traveled through the Orient and Europe before returning to the United States in 1858, but he did not come West again until 1862. This time, his tour was a triumph bringing an extra benefit when he renewed his friendship with Sarah Stark. They were married in 1883 and lived in the East until his death in 1893.

Another actor in Booth's company of 1851, J.J. McCloskey, made a brief but substantial name for himself both at the Jenny Lind and in Stark's company, where he played in *Macbeth*. When

4. Marysville Herald, *January 25, 1854.*

that season ended in the spring of 1852, he took a troupe on a tour of the mines, collecting good reviews along with full houses, and by October, 1852, even suspicious Marysville was "in ecstasies" over him.[5] After a year and a half with the Thornes, he spent the early part of 1855 in Catherine Sinclair's company, then returned permanently to the East.

J.D. ("Ned") McGowan was hailed as "an actor of considerable merit" when he made his San Francisco debut in the Proctor/Stark *Merchant of Venice* in January, 1853.[6] He was an immediate favorite, highly praised for his Ghost in Murdoch's *Hamlet* and for Friar Laurence in *Romeo and Juliet*. He toured almost constantly until December, 1854, when he returned to San Francisco to play a few weeks in Neafie's company. As soon as the season ended, he set off again, acting for Kent and for the Chapmans before assembling his own touring troupe in May, 1855. That tour ended abruptly in Napa when he was charged with the murder of James King. Although he was completely exonerated, he abandoned management. He continued to act, however, and won glowing praises for his Shylock in a Nevada City production of *Merchant of Venice* in 1856. Eventually, he made his way back to San Francisco, where he co-managed and performed as leading man with Rowena Granice in October, 1857. By this time, he was ready to return east, and 1857 was his last recorded appearance in California.

One of the best known leading men was the handsome, accomplished Charles Wheatleigh, who came to California at the behest of Laura Keene, although he was not with her in the beginning. On her arrival in April, 1854, she chose Edwin Booth to play opposite her, but when the reviews were less than rhapsodic, she blamed him and sent for Wheatleigh. He reached San Francisco in July to play Benedick in her *Much Ado about Nothing*. Audiences approved of his "admirable manner" and pronounced him "an ornament to his profession."[7]

For some reason (possibly Keene's temperament), it was

5. Mountain Echo, *October 9, 1852.*
6. Golden Era, *January 10, 1853.*
7. Golden Era, *July 16, 1854.*

Booth, not Wheatleigh, who accompanied her to Australia. Wheatleigh remained in San Francisco, supporting the Starks, Neafie, and Jean Davenport until Keene's return in 1855. As her leading man once more, he was commended for his "excellent" Malvolio in *Twelfth Night,* Orlando in *As You Like It,* and one of the Antipholuses in *Comedy of Errors,* but when Keene returned east, he went with her.

One of the Dromios in *Comedy of Errors* was William Henry Sedley, son of the Welsh actor Harry Smith. When he first went on the stage, he called himself "W.H. Sedley," but before long he changed it to "W.H. Smith," perhaps to capitalize on his father's fame. He began as a leading man, making his debut as Hamlet in San Francisco on December 26, 1854. His dark good looks and dashing manner made him a popular favorite, and he had a long career, beginning with major roles in Laura Keene's 1855 Shakespeare series. In Jean Davenport's company some time later, his Romeo received higher marks than her Juliet, and in March, 1858, he was a "formal but pleasing" Florizel in the Wallack production of *The Winter's Tale.* He left San Francisco after that but only to become a manager and settle in California. He loved acting and was one of the few to make the transition into character roles, possibly because he was always best at comedy. His last appearances were as comic old men.

While leading men were expected to play comedy, those who hoped to become stars preferred tragic roles. Such a one was James Warwick, whom Walter Leman succinctly described as an "aspiring tragedian." Warwick came to California in 1854 and played in San Francisco with Wheatleigh and Sarah Stark until the summer of 1855, when he joined the Neafie-Potter company. For six years, he toured almost continuously with indifferent success. His Mercutio in Annette Ince's *Romeo and Juliet* was poorly received, as were Shylock and Hamlet in his own troupe. As his status declined, he acted in lesser companies: the Sierra company; the Star, and George Mitchell's "equestrian company," promising audiences he would "lay his bones" in each of the 58 camps they visited, but in 1860, after a final performance of *Hamlet* in Nevada City, he took his bones eastward.

Popularity could be gained fairly quickly, but a good reputation required several years of constant playing. Few Easterners were willing to give that much time to the West after 1856, when gold was no longer lavishly expended by happy-go-lucky prospectors. Leading players anxious to become stars spent less and less time in California. W.H. Fleming, who acted from February to May 1857 as leading man to Mary Provost, Harriet Carpenter, and Annette Ince, made an excellent impression in standard roles, but when he attempted Romeo for Annette Ince's Juliet, he was soundly censured and went home.

Fewer women became leading players in their own right. Contemporary plays were written for female stars, but Shakespearean women's roles were subordinate to men's. Most often, for economic reasons, the leading woman was the leading man's wife, whether or not she was particularly talented. Sometimes ingenues served as temporary substitutes, sometimes character women, but a wise leading man knew the value of a strong actress opposite him, and good leading women were in demand throughout their short careers.

In the Jenny Lind company of 1851, the bright young ingenue Kate Grey was already a skilled comedienne admired for her "piquancy and aptitude."[8] She soon graduated to leading woman roles and began a series of tours, appearing in Downieville with J.J. McCloskey in 1852 and in Nevada City with the Wallers in 1853. Toward the end of that year, she was in Neafie's San Francisco company, but the next year she was back touring with Jean Davenport and from 1855 to 1857 with Estelle Potter. She starred for a time at Scott's Bar until she was thrown by a horse and spent several months recuperating from a broken arm. Like most leading women, her acting life ended with the bloom of youth, and her last recorded appearance was in Phelps's Sierra Company of 1857.

Julia Pelby, daughter of a Boston theater manager, was another who developed from ingenue into leading woman. She came to California in 1853, and during her first year acted at the Metropolitan in San Francisco and with the Starks in Sacramento. In 1855, touring with A.H. Phelps, James Warwick, and the

8. Evening Picayune, *October 13, 1851.*

Chapmans, she made enough of a reputation to travel at the head of a company managed by Jacob Wonderley Thoman.

She and Thoman were married in Oregon that year and came back to San Francisco, where she played Luciana in Laura Keene's *Comedy of Errors,* then, as the star of her husband's Union Dramatic Troupe, toured the state for three years. She was so popular that in January, 1858, Wesley Venua featured her in his Sacramento company and soon after, Stark engaged her as his leading lady. It was more profitable, however, to star in her husband's company, and for the next ten years the Thomans toured California. In 1868, they returned to her home town of Boston, hoping the East would receive her as warmly as the West had, but before she could make her first appearance, she was injured in a fall. To ease the pain, she took laudanum, the standard pain killer of the time, and on December 8, 1868, an accidental overdose caused her death.

Australia sent many stars to California but even more journeymen performers. One of the better of these was Marie Duret, who was in Catherine Sinclair's Metropolitan company of 1853 and spent the next five years touring the mines. As a leading lady in various troupes, she played most often in contemporary plays, but according to the Nevada City papers, she was superb as Romeo in an 1856 production of *Romeo and Juliet.* In 1859, she returned to Australia for several years. A second visit to California in 1864 was not as successful as the first, and after a two-character production of *Hamlet* in Virginia City was severely criticized, she left for home.

When Marie Duret played Romeo, her Juliet was another Australian, the incomparable Sophie Edwin. Born in Sydney and brought to San Francisco by her parents in 1850, she made her stage debut at the Jenny Lind the following year as a twelve-year-old ingenue. In 1853, Frederick Kent and his wife took her into their touring company as leading lady, and within two years she had become such a favorite that Catherine Sinclair cast her in *Much Ado about Nothing* and as Gertrude in Edwin Booth's *Hamlet.* When she appeared alone, she often starred, but she also supported major stars like Neafie, Julia Dean Hayne, Annette Ince, J.E. McDonough, and Jean Davenport. The *Herald* critic called her "full of archness and attractive, womanly delicacy,"[9] and Walter Leman, who often worked with her, paid an even greater compliment:

> As an emotional actress, she was not far behind the foremost of her profession, and there was a sympathy in her voice that touched a sympathetic chord in the heart of every listener.[10]

When she died at the age of thirty-eight, she was one of California's most brilliant and beloved actresses.

An actress who began as a leading lady was Mrs. Claughley, first noted as the "reigning star" of Marysville in January, 1853.[11] She stayed there for over a year, playing opposite James Murdoch and supporting Laura Keene, until the following year when Keene brought her to San Francisco. She must have had a good repertory, for in December, 1854, Stark cast her in *King John, Macbeth, Othello, Merry Wives of Windsor, Midsummer Night's Dream,* and *Pericles,* and the following year, she played Lesbia in Laura Keene's *Comedy of Errors.* In 1858, she acted Paulina in James Wallack's production of *The Winter's Tale,* but the critics considered her "poor,"[12] and apparently she retired, for her name is not mentioned again.

Rowena Granice also began as a leading woman, playing Desdemona in John Edwin McDonough's 1857 production of *Othello,* and D.V. Gates was so impressed with her performance that he took her into his touring company. She charmed audiences from the beginning, and wherever she went she was given special marks of favor. Miners threw bags of gold to her, and Oroville gave her a belt with a gold buckle. She was more than just an actress, however, and she soon went into management in Sacramento, where audiences were pleased by her taste in plays and her choice of stars. With the depression of 1856, however, box office receipts fell, and Granice moved to San Francisco to manage the Union Theater with Ned McGowan as her leading man until he

9. *Gagey, p. 79, quoting the* Herald.
10. *Leman, pp. 256–57.*
11. Golden Era, *January 30, 1853.*
12. Golden Era, *March 15, 1858.*

left for the East. In the meantime, she met the "Yankee comedian," J.P. Addams, and early in 1858 began a tour with him as her star. A few months later, they were married. They continued their highly profitable tours until 1860, when they returned to the East.

As noted earlier, husband and wife teams of equal stature were not the rule, but the Conners were an exception. Edmund S. Conner was a typical leading man, exceptionally handsome with a fine voice and excellent speech; he was a "good but not great" ac- tor.[13] Born in Tennessee, he made his debut in New York in 1833 and had played the major theaters from Boston to New Orleans. His wife, born Charlotte Barnes, was the daughter of an acting family and began her stage career as a child. In spite of a plain face and a weak voice, she was popular with audiences, and the pair met with considerable success.

Frederick Kent first presented them on March 4, 1855, in Marysville, but within a month they were out on tour. They had a good supply of Shakespeare in their repertory and they played it often, particularly *Macbeth*, a favorite in the smaller towns like Nevada City, and for four years Marysville, Oroville, and the mountain camps hailed them warmly and kept close track of their actions. When Edmund became ill in September, 1857, it was news, and his recovery was duly noted along with the hope that he would be back onstage soon. Their home was in the East, however, and by the end of 1858 they were ready to return. After Charlotte gave a series of Shakespeare readings in San Francisco, they made their way to Victoria and sailed for New York.

Leading men and women were good workmanlike performers, proud of their profession. They were what most people visualized when they thought of "actors"—handsome, graceful and charming, not surrounded by the mysterious untouchable aura of the stars but, with some allowance for theatrical oddity, essentially of the people.

## *Juveniles and Ingenues*

Juveniles and ingenues were often beginners, attractive youngsters without much experience. They played in the subplot

13. *Leman, p. 247.*

or the lesser love interest, and generally their parts were fairly simple; they merely had to speak and move reasonably well. If they
were more than just adequate, however, they might graduate to
leading men and women.

Two veterans of the Mexican war played the juvenile roles in
Atwater's company: John ("Jack") Harris, from Major Graham's
dragoons, and Lieutenant Wright, from Stevenson's Volunteers.
After the Eagle company disbanded, Harris spent his time touring
until 1854, when he went to Australia. Wright stayed in San Francisco and joined June Booth's company, where he played a "very
good" Duncan in Booth's *Macbeth.* He then toured with J.J.
McCloskey's company in 1852, playing Othello in Downieville
before returning to act Kent in Stark's *King Lear* of 1853. After a
season with Neafie in Sacramento in 1855, he vanishes from the
playbills.

Juveniles were rarely outstanding, but in the early years
critics were fairly kind to them. Young Byers was scolded for his
bad elocution in Stark's *Macbeth* and *Hamlet,* but the criticism was
softened at the end, "We remind him of these things in hopes of
seeing an improvement; not for the purpose of condemning him
as an actor."[14] Byers did not stay long in San Francisco. In 1852,
he toured in McCloskey's company, in 1853 with the Chapmans,
and then he left the stage.

An actor of more endurance was the Australian Henry Coad,
who came to California with Nesbit McCron in 1850 and stayed
on when most of the company returned home. In the Stark company of 1851, he was a literal as well as figurative target of John
Hambleton's jealousy over Mrs. Hambleton's friendship with him;
Hambleton tried to shoot Coad and was out searching for him
when his wife committed suicide. In the charges and counter-
charges that followed, however, Coad seems to have been regarded
by both sides as an innocent bystander and no blame was attached
to him.

He remained in California until 1857, a popular actor who
played in most of the major companies and almost always received
special attention for his performance. In 1853, critics praised his

14. Evening Picayune, *December 10, 1851.*

Mercutio in the Murdoch-Baker production of *Romeo and Juliet* and his Don Pedro in *Much Ado about Nothing.* During the following two years, he was a principal player in San Francisco theaters managed by Catherine Sinclair, Laura Keene, and J.A. Neafie. In 1856, he acted in Frederick Kent's touring company, but by March, 1857, he was back in San Francisco playing Cassio in McDonough's *Othello* at the Metropolitan. Shortly afterwards, he was in Annette Ince's company at the same theater, but by then San Francisco was in the throes of a serious depression, and attendance suffered. Actors now paid twenty-five shillings a week, "sighed for the times when the commonest *supers* on our boards commanded a salary of a 'slug' a week."[15] Coad solved his economic problems by going to China. He returned to San Francisco in 1859 but only for a few months before sailing home to Australia.

A juvenile who might have become a California star was C.A. King. He first appeared as a member of Stark's company in the 1852–53 season, drawing high praise for his Cassio in the Proctor-Stark *Othello*. He was also a stage-manager and proved so skillful that in 1854 Joshua Proctor chose him to co-manage his touring company, and the next year George Ryer asked him to co-manage his Sacramento theater. Later, King went into solo management with a touring company and became celebrated for choosing the best actors available and for producing fine shows. Actors so appreciated his habit of rewarding especially good performances with gifts[16] that after his sudden death in 1857, they gave a benefit to raise money for a monument in his name.

Playing juveniles not only provided an entry into the theater, it was also a weeding out process. Henry Coad and C.A. King were rare youngsters who developed beyond the first step, one as an actor, the other as a manager. The majority of juveniles, like Harris, Wright, and Byers, acted for a few years, then left the theater.

Typical of this kind were Mr. Wilder (first name never given) and Samuel B. Leaman. Wilder acted in Stark's company during

---

15. Golden Era, *July 5, 1857.*

16. *In Marysville, he gave George Ryer a gold-headed manzanita cane.* Golden Era, *January 7, 1855.*

1852. He played Ludovico in the Proctor-Stark *Othello* and Horatio in Edwin Booth's *Hamlet,* supported James Murdoch in 1853 and Laura Keene in 1854, then spent three years touring the mining camps. His last California season was 1857–58 in San Francisco, playing a minor role in Julia Dean Hayne's *Henry VIII.* Leaman, another juvenile in that production, began with great promise but apparently was an alcoholic. Only a few months after *Henry VIII,* he was a suicide, drowned in San Francisco Bay at the age of twenty-seven.

Like juveniles, ingenues seldom lasted long. Either they developed fairly quickly into leading women or they left the profession. They were distinguished from the soubrettes who, although equally young, were essentially character women with a bent for comedy. The ingenue role, on the other hand, was the sweet young thing, helpless, unworldly, and quite innocent. Contemporary playwrights nearly always wrote a character of this kind into their dramas; in Shakespeare, they played such roles as Celia in *As You Like It,* Olivia in *Twelfth Night,* or, if a star was unavailable, Desdemona and Juliet.

Nesbit McCron's Desdemona, Mme. Duprez, had been highly approved in her San Francisco debut during the fall of 1850, when she acted in contemporary plays, but when she attempted *Othello,* she was charged with "murdering the part."[17] She was more successful in James Stark's *Othello,* and the critic unbent enough to say, "This lady has good abilities, and needs only to know her part well to act it well," although he added a warning that in the future he would "mark, kindly, what we consider faults."[18] She was in the Starks' company after the Hambleton debacle and played male roles for a few days, because there were not enough men. For unknown reasons, she attempted suicide a week later but recovered enough to continue her career until at least 1854, when she was last noted as the ingenue at Mokelumne Hill.

Even more ephemeral was the career of Miss Montague, who entered the Jenny Lind company at the same time as Kate Grey. She was an excellent "First Singing Witch" in Stark's *Macbeth* and

17. *MacMinn, p. 80.*
18. Alta California, *January 2, 1851.*

did "exceedingly well" as Ophelia in his *Hamlet*.[19] She continued to play young supporting roles until 1857 when, apparently, she retired.

An American actress, Emily Coad (no relation to Henry Coad), was brought from New Orleans by June Booth in 1852. Although she stayed only a year and a half, she was a favorite player in his Jenny Lind company, in the Bakers' troupe, and on the road with J.J. McCloskey. Her last performance before going back to New York was as Ophelia to James Murdoch's Hamlet. In the East, she specialized in burlesque Shakespeare, particularly Portia, and, after a successful engagement in England, settled there permanently in 1873.

Although the career of Anna Smith, wife of W.H. Smith, lasted only four years, it was unusual, for she played both soubrettes and ingenues. She not only acted with her husband but in Sacramento companies by herself—for Neafie and Estelle Potter in 1854 and for both Venua and Shaw in 1858—before retiring to family life.

A gifted ingenue with a ten-year career was Fanny Howard. Her first notice came in Neafie's San Francisco company of 1854, where she played for one season. The following year, she toured with Catherine Sinclair and was a popular player in other companies for three years. In 1857, she gave solo Shakespeare readings in Sacramento, but most of her career was spent on tour. She was versatile enough to play Emilia in *Othello* as well as Juliet, and one story about a disrupted performance indicates the kind of audiences she met. The play was *Romeo and Juliet,* given in Virginia City in 1864. In the midst of the potion scene, she had just spoken the line, "What if this mixture do not work at all?" when a small boy in the audience shouted, "Take a dose of pills!"[20] For the audience, the tragedy ended there.

For obvious reasons, the ingenue's career was apt to be even less enduring than the juvenile's, and the turnover was greater than for any other category. Often they were youngsters attracted by the stage only until they discovered its discipline and discom-

---

19. Evening Picayune, *December 18 and 19, 1851.*
20. *Watson, p. 270 and note.*

forts. Some, like Fanny Morgan, who starred in the Shakespeare tricentennial performance of *Midsummer Night's Dream* on April 23, 1864, played just once. Many acted only a few times, others married and left the stage, few stayed long enough to make a name for themselves or to become leading women. Yet, since every play required at least one young couple, there was a great demand for their services. It was indeed fortunate that, no matter how rapidly they came and went, the supply was constantly replenished.

## *Character Players*

Character men and women could be of any age, and they were not necessarily physically attractive. They had longer careers than other types, because aging mattered less and because their range was necessarily broader. They could become stars, but the way was harder and required a distinctly recognizable specialty. While leading men and women found it extremely difficult to switch from major to minor roles, character players usually began and ended in supporting parts.

One of the most notable actors in this line was Ned Bingham, who, with John Harris, had been in Major Graham's dragoons. After leaving Monterey in 1850, he and his wife joined the short-lived company of Nesbit McCron, played briefly in Stockton, then returned to San Francisco, where James Stark and Sarah Kirby engaged them at the Jenny Lind. They were already fairly well known, and on November 18, 1851, the *Evening Picayune* announced their first appearance with, "Hundreds will go to greet their old favorite, Mrs. Bingham."

They were not great actors, and the newspapers let them know when they failed to meet expectations. In *Black Eyed Susan,* Bingham was sharply told to, "bear in mind that the audience are as much interested in *understanding* what he says, as he is in saying it. Muttering sounds without articulation is not acting."[21] In *Six Degrees of Crime,* Mrs. Bingham was scolded for wearing "flashy red

21. Evening Picayune, *November 20, 1851.*

shoes" when she was supposed to be in mourning,[22] and as Regan in Stark's *King Lear* she was "to apt to play as though she had just so much to say, and was in a hurry to get through it."[23] Still, they were well-liked. Bingham joined the volunteer fire department, and when Sarah Stark tried to dismiss him after a quarrel, the firemen tore up the theater. He was quickly reinstated, and the quarrel evidently resolved, for when the Starks went to Sacramento at the end of the season, Bingham took over the management.

In the summer of 1852, the Binghams enlarged their following, particularly in Downieville and Marysville, by touring with J.J. McCloskey. The tour, however, ended on a grim note with the death of Mrs. Bingham in the autumn. When the saddened Bingham returned briefly to San Francisco, he acted for June Booth and for James Stark. In January, 1853, he played Brabantio in Stark's *Othello,* then returned to Marysville, where he spent the rest of that year and the first part of 1854 managing the theater. He came back to San Francisco in February, 1854, to play in the Bakers' company; after they went East, he stayed on to manage the American with C.F. Thorne, but in a few weeks, Marysville called him to manage there again, and he moved back.

In August, 1854, he set off for the East, but something terrible seems to have happened to him. The *Marysville Herald* reported that he had been murdered in Aspinwall, Panama. It was not true, but other stories confirmed that all was not well. One rumor held that he had not left San Francisco but was seriously ill on a steamship there, another said he did sail but while at sea was beaten by male passengers on the ship when he "tried to cultivate a friendship" with Mrs. Woodward, who was then returning to the East, and still another asserted that he joined a Central American army and was badly wounded. Whatever the truth, he returned to California in 1857, partially paralyzed, his health permanently impaired.

The Metropolitan company gave him a benefit on March 22, and, although the audience was only "fair," he received over $200.[24] He and his daughter moved to Marysville, where he leased

22. Evening Picayune, *November 22, 1851.*
23. Evening Picayune, *December 20–21, 1851.*
24. Golden Era, *March 22, 1857.*

the theater for a few weeks, but evidently the strain of management was too great, for a month later, he was the proprietor of a cigar stand in the barroom of Hann House Hotel. He wrote a play, *The Siege of Grenada,* that was performed first in Marysville and then in Sacramento in the summer of 1856. Miss Albertine acted the heroine, Bingham played a crippled solider and his daughter one of the small roles. It played two nights to small houses.[25] Two more benefits this year, one in September by Annette Ince and one in December at Maguire's Opera House, replenished his purse, but he spent the rest of his days more or less retired.

Another early character actor was D.G. Robinson's partner, J. Evrard. In 1850, they opened the Dramatic Museum in San Francisco, and it was Evrard who kept the theater going during Robinson's frequent absence on tour. He was not the best of managers, and in September, 1850, he had to take a benefit to make ends meet. In October, 1851, he gave up and entered June Booth's company at the Jenny Lind. He was a "judicious, indefatigable" player, with enough Shakespeare in his repertory for Booth to cast him in *Richard III* and Stark in *Hamlet* and *Macbeth* in their 1852 seasons. He and Mrs. Evrard were in Booth's Jenny Lind company in January, 1852, but apparently he died soon after, for only her name appears after that time. She played in Neafie's Sacramento company in 1855 and, for the last recorded time, in Miss Albertine's Lyceum company of 1858.

When the Jenny Lind opened its doors on October 4, 1851, the first line was spoken by the English actor Wesley Venua, already of some note in New York and New Orleans. He demonstrated his training in his "chaste and correct" support of Booth's *Richard III,* as Banquo in *Macbeth,* and as Horatio when Booth presented Stark in *Hamlet.* He was an uneven actor, however, and a few days later, another performance of Banquo brought the reproof that he played it "without the least animation."[26]

In spite of his habit of cooking tripe backstage, he was popular with his fellow players, and he worked almost constantly. Proctor hired him for the 1852–53 season, and he not only played Roderigo

25. Golden Era, *June 21 and August 2, 1857.*
26. Evening Picayune, *December 19, 1851.*

in the Proctor-Stark *Othello,* but assisted in the management. He was most often in touring companies: in April, 1855, with Jean Davenport, in November, 1855, with Catherine Sinclair, in 1857 with Mary Provost, and in 1859 with Annette Ince. Between the last two engagements, he stayed mostly in Sacramento where, in January, 1858, he managed a company. It was not a success, and within a month, he went back to acting. His name disappears from the records after 1860.

George Mitchell, like Venua, was also in Booth's first company. He started poorly when critics complained he did not learn his lines, but within two months, his Polonius in Stark's *Hamlet* "showed marked improvement,"[27] and his performance in *Macbeth* a few nights later was noted as "good." In the spring of 1852, the Jenny Lind season having ended, he gathered a company and started off for the mining camps. He had a fair, though not outstanding, troupe, and they played to full houses. Encouraged by this success, Mitchell did not return to San Francisco but continued to tour throughout the next few years. By 1855, however, the competition of circuses, minstrels, and musical groups made such inroads on the box office that he needed to find a new way to attract audiences, and he formed an "equestrian" company. Leman, who played one season with him, says they traveled with one horse and a small wagon. Business continued so poor that for a time Mitchell gave up managing and acted in other companies, but in 1858, he went back to managing his own "Dramatico-Equestrian Company." After a last tour of Fiddletown, Volcano, Drytown, Jackson, and Ione Valley, he returned to the East.

One of the best character actors was George Spear who learned his craft in the Pelby company of Boston. A close friend and drinking partner of Junius Brutus Booth, he came to San Francisco with him in July, 1852, and stayed on to watch over Edwin during his first season with Waller. From his earliest days he was called "Old Spear" and almost always played old men, although, like most supporting actors, he was adaptable to many different kinds of roles and acted with most of the stars who came west, including Laura Keene, Neafie, Warwick's "equestrian" troupe, and the

27. Evening Picayune, *December 12, 1851.*

ubiquitous John Potter. He returned east in 1856 and nine years later was playing in Laura Keene's company of *Our American Cousin* the night Lincoln was assassinated.

Another genuinely gifted actor was David Anderson, whose range was narrow, but who was called "the very best delineator of 'old men' we have ever had in California."[28] His nickname, "Old Spudge," contrasted strongly with his physical appearance, for he was tall and thin, with refined features, an aristocratic bearing, and cultivated manners. Trained in New York, he had played New Orleans several times before coming to California in 1850. He first acted the Ghost in Stark's *Hamlet* but was soon found to be a much greater Polonius. As a "comic old man," he toured in Stark's company and in Waller's, where he became a close friend of the young Edwin Booth. Back in San Francisco they shared living quarters, acted in Sinclair's company, and went to Australia together in 1854. When he returned, he was outstanding as Kent in Stark's *King Lear* and as Old Adam in *As You Like It.* When Booth went east in 1856, Anderson stayed on, toured with Mary Provost, went bankrupt managing his own company, and returned to acting in Annette Ince's company. In 1858, after an engagement for Matilda Wood and a last tour with James Anderson, he went home to the East.

Certain actors, like George Ryer, changed after coming west. A short, thickset man, he was best in comedy but preferred serious roles like Hamlet and Richard III, and on his arrival in San Francisco in 1853, billed himself as a "tragedian." After acting with Neafie and with Jean Davenport, with whom he also toured, he took over the Stockton theater in 1854 and discovered he had a distinct talent for management. Two years later, he made a short tour with Catherine Sinclair, then returned to San Francisco to manage Julia Dean Hayne's company. In 1857, he teamed up with Estelle Potter in a travelling company for several months, then, except for a brief season with the Wallack company in 1859, managed for Annette Ince until she went east. In 1860, he and James Stark toured with a troupe that went as far south as Los Angeles before returning to Marysville. Here, in the fall, they organized a troupe

28. Golden Era, *February 27, 1853.*

to play agricultural fairs. Somewhat later, Ryer underwent still another change, retired from the theater and became an army chaplain.

Far from the most colorful but certainly among the most likable was the gentle, affable character actor Walter Leman who left a rich history of the times and warm recollections of his fellow players in his *Memories of an Old Actor.* Born in New England, he began his career in Boston, and by 1854, when he started west, his reputation as an actor "of some distinction" was well established in Louisville, St. Louis, and New Orleans.[29]

In California, he spent some time in Sacramento and Marysville before going to San Francisco, where he managed the American until Laura Keene arrived. She was her own manager, but she hired Leman for her company; he played Sir Toby Belch in *Twelfth Night,* Jaques in *As You Like It,* and Aegeon in *Comedy of Errors.* He was always in demand, and during the last months of 1855 into January 1856, he toured. In Nevada City, he played Mercutio in the Duret-Edwin *Romeo and Juliet,* a part he repeated when he returned to Sacramento as part of Catherine Sinclair's company, where he also played the Ghost to Edwin Booth's Hamlet.

He was probably popular because he was not only a good actor but often seen on California stages. In 1856, he toured with McKean Buchanan and in 1857 with Annette Ince; between April 8 and June 7, 1858, he travelled over 1,000 miles and played fifty-eight towns with George Mitchell's "equestrian company." Yet he never complained and described touring in glowing terms:

> a party of us would anticipate the coach departure, and tramp it over hill and through valley in the balmy morning air, or leave the carriage and take a cut-off trail beneath the shadow of mountain pines redolent with spicy odors, gaining perhaps a half hour's time, which would be spent upon the grass in company with a cigar, while we waited for the coach to come up. In the solemn silence of those forest hills, no sound would be heard save the woodpecker and the soughing of the wind amid the branches of

29. Golden Era, *January 7, 1855.*

the tall tree tops — till anon, a subdued rattle of wheels slowly coming up the grade in the distance. The driver coming in sight would crack his whip, the ladies in the coach wave their handkerchiefs, and on reaching the summit the horses rest and take a drink, and reseating ourselves in the coach we would roll merrily on.[30]

He says little of the dangers, although they were common enough. Quite apart from wild animals, unfriendly Indians, fires, floods, and massive storms, the towns themselves were full of armed men, often drunk, as he learned in Virginia City where his room was over the bar. Leman was quietly preparing for bed when a quarrel below nearly ended his life as a bullet whizzed through the thin floorboards, grazed his ear and buried itself in the ceiling. Not long after, he left for Hawaii where he restored his nerves before resuming his career in the East.

Among the character women, Mrs. Mansfield, known for her "amiability and lady-like deportment,"[31] was a favorite. She was both well trained and versatile, with a long career in New York before she came to California in 1850. Like Mlle. Duret, she played men's roles in Stark's company after Mrs. Hambleton's suicide, but she was primarily a character actress, a strong support for stars. In July, 1853, she was in J.J. McCloskey's company in Downieville, where she played Emilia for Wright's *Othello,* and he showed his appreciation by giving her a special benefit before she returned to San Francisco. There she acted in Proctor's troupe in December 1853, but a month later set off on tour, moving from Ben Moulton's troupe to Frederick Kent's to Warwick's "Equestrian" company in Sacramento. At the end of that engagement, she went east and did not return.

One of June Booth's best choices for the Jenny Lind company was the forceful character actress known only as Mrs. Woodward. Her "bold and queenlike actions" made her an excellent Elizabeth in *Richard III,* while her highly favored Lady Macbeth was considered "right in every respect."[32] During her first year and a half in California, she acted mostly in San Francisco with Booth,

30. *Leman, 274–75.*
31. Mountain Echo, *August 7, 1853.*
32. Evening Picayune, *November 29, 1851.*

Joshua Proctor, and the Starks, but in the fall of 1852, she ventured out as far as Marysville. When she closed there, it was as a "popular tragic actress" with "hosts of admirers."[33] She returned to San Francisco, acted at the Metropolitan, briefly managed the Union with Sarah Stark, then announced she was going back to the Eastern stage. She left that summer on the same ship as the unfortunate Ned Bingham and became the subject of one speculation about his injuries.[34]

Not all players went back to the East. Some, like Mrs. Judah, found a permanent home in California. Born Marietta Starfield, she was a character actress from the beginning and might have spent her entire career as a "utility woman," never a star but always working. Her life took a dramatic change, however, when she married actor Emmanuel Judah. Together with their two childen, they went to Florida and, after a time, set off for Cuba. On the way, the ship was wrecked, Judah and the children drowned.

She went on acting, keeping the name Judah although in 1847 she married John Torrence, a stagehand. In 1852, they moved west to California where, at the age of forty, she entered the Jenny Lind company. Within a few months of her arrival, she was considered as "a head and shoulders above them all,"[35] an artist equal to any star. Her illness in the summer of 1854 was a matter of anxious public concern and her recovery reported with relief; the Bakers were so delighted to have her back that the company presented her with a 77-piece tea set.

Perhaps her greatest asset was her versatility. She could play a powerful Lady Macbeth for Neafie, a jaded Prudence in Jean Davenport's *Camille,* a deliciously comic Maria in Laura Keene's *Twelfth Night,* or a gentle Abbess in *Comedy of Errors* with equal skill. Both in San Francisco and on tour she acted with Annette Ince, Julia Dean Hayne, John Edwin McDonough, and Matilda Wood. In 1858, San Franciscans were enthusiastically urged to support a benefit for her, because she had "for over six years been an especial

33. Golden Era, *January 16, 1853.*

34. *It has been suggested that this Mrs. Woodward was Susan Denin, who also married a Mr. Woodward. Susan Denin Woodward, however, was touring California in 1854.*

35. Golden Era, *January 1, 1854.*

benefit" to them,[36] and they responded with a full house. When she was out of Matilda Wood's company because of illness, her absence "left a void" that could not be filled by anyone else.

Although she acted a wide range of parts, she was particularly good as Gertrude in Murdoch's *Hamlet* and as the Nurse in the Bakers' *Romeo and Juliet.* Of the latter character, Walter Leman says:

> I think no "Juliet" every played in San Francisco that was not overshadowed by the "Nurse" of Mrs. Judah, and her appearance even in a most insignificant role was always signalized by hearty applause.[37]

Her career as a character actress was a long one. She stayed in California, acting well into her sixties, and when she observed her silver wedding anniversary in 1872, the entire theatrical community celebrated. She died in her adopted city in 1883.

By the nature of their roles, character actors had less recognition than leading actors, and many are recalled only from memoirs or stories about events concerning them. Leman, for example, draws little thumbnail sketches of actors never mentioned in the papers: Joseph Smith, known as "Little Smithy," who managed to remain immaculate at all times, the "careless, reckless, laughing soul" of "Rascal Jack" Dunn, and "Dumpsy" Dumphries, who once played *Richard III* while riding on a jackass. The affection they inspired in their audiences was deep and lasting, but aside from such fond memories, they had to be satisfied with such transient recognition as the applause at the end of a performance.

## Comics

Male character actors with a bent for humor often became comics, divided into high and low. High comics played genteel characters and fops, low comics were closer to clowns. Young

36. Golden Era, *February 28, 1858.*
37. Leman, *pp. 236–237.*

character actresses played soubrette roles — flirts or the comedy ingenue — but they also acted in serious plays. As they grew older, they played spinster aunts, mothers, grandmothers and old hags, depending on their qualifications.

Atwater's low comedian was the Australian Henry Ray. Mrs. Ray, "of the Theatre Royal, New Zealand," played all the women's roles, but she was probably a soubrette. She was greatly admired, in spite of her Down Under accent that sounded like Cockney and gave a comic touch to her speech when she intoned such lines as, "Me 'ope, me 'ope, me honly 'ope!" After the Eagle company dissolved, the Rays joined Nesbit McCron's Australian troupe for a few weeks and went home. The other Atwater comedian was Tench Fairchild, who gave up acting for scene painting. In a sense, he was responsible for Edwin Booth's Shakespearean debut; when June Booth gave him a benefit in 1853, he insisted young Booth play *Richard III* for it.

A very early actor-manager, D.G. Robinson, opened the Dramatic Museum in San Francisco on July 4, 1850, with his actor partner, J. Evrard. As managers, they were no match for Thomas Maguire, and the Dramatic Museum closed in February, 1852. They might have been more successful if their hearts had not been in acting. Robinson spent the summer of 1851 on tour, playing to full houses in Marysville and Nevada City. He was a comedian specializing in "Yankee" characters, but he was versatile enough to play with the Chapmans in their parody of *Richard III* in June, 1853, to perform his own *Hamlet Travestie* in December of that year, and for Laura Keene to use him in her Shakespeare series of June, 1854. For the most part, however, he acted standard comedy until his death of fever in 1856.[38]

Frederick M. Kent was just twenty-two and had just made his debut in his native Philadelphia when Booth invited him to California. In the Jenny Lind company, he specialized in low comedy, and the *Evening Picayune* once remarked that "his appearance on the stage is the signal for a smile," but he could also play serious roles in Stark's 1851 productions of *Hamlet* and *Macbeth*. The following year he played Touchstone in the Bakers' *As You Like It,* a role

38. *Gagey, p. 78.*

he repeated in Laura Keene's 1855 production. Between these engagements, he married a gifted young comedienne, Jennie Parker, and toured. The two were soon among the most popular players in the mining towns, their appearances announced weeks before their arrival.

In 1855, Kent managed a successful three-month season in Marysville, then moved to San Francisco to play Andrew Aguecheek in Laura Keene's *Twelfth Night* and "Dr. Punch" in *Comedy of Errors* as well as Touchstone in *As You Like It.* In spite of high praises, he did not feel he did well in the West, and soon after the end of Keene's season, he took his wife back to New York. Here, he did even less well, and he never fulfilled his early promise. Increasing bouts with alcohol impaired his performances long before his death in January, 1858.

Few actors had such gifts. While they had to be ready for any kind of part, most developed a clear specialty. A.H. Phelps, who acted in California for five years, generally played genteel comedy. He first appeared in San Francisco in 1853; the next year he played in Laura Keene's company and played Macduff in Neafie's *Macbeth.* When Stark returned from Australia in 1854, Phelps supported him as Laertes in *Hamlet,* then spent another two years touring. These slapdash performances may have had a deleterious effect on his acting, for when he played in Ince's San Francisco company in 1857, he was severely criticized as "about the worst actor we have ever had," and "essentially an eccentric comedian," whose tragedy and melodrama were "unbearable."[39] He spent his last two years in California outside of San Francisco, visiting the friendlier mining camps — Nevada City even *liked* his Hamlet.

Romance as well as tragedy flourished backstage. Close relationships with outsiders were difficult, partly because of actors' constant travels, partly because of the "immoral" reputation attached to the theater. For the most part, players married within the profession and, although divorce was somewhat more common than in the settled communities, most stayed together. Two who met and married in California were Jacob Wonderley Thoman and Julia Pelby (see page 136 above).

39. Golden Era, *November 15 and 22, 1857.*

Thoman was born in Philadelphia, where he made his debut and spent the early years of his career. He married actress Elizabeth Anderson, came west in 1853, and joined the Bakers' company, where he played low comedy as one of the Dromios in *Comedy of Errors,* Peter in *Romeo and Juliet,* and Dogberry in *Much Ado About Nothing.* His wife divorced him, remarried and retired; Thoman stayed in San Francisco for about a year, acted in Neafie's company, where he met Julia Pelby, toured with her, and finally married her. He managed her career in California and was preparing to do the same in the East when she died. He did not come back to California.

Every company needed a low comedian, and one of the best was William Barry, who came west in 1852. He may have used the overland route, for he acted in Nevada City before he went to San Francisco's Metropolitan in 1853. He toured with Stark, Waller, Jean Davenport, Mary Provost, and Annette Ince and was regarded as "about the best" in his line.[40] Some insight on the approach to the nineteenth-century *King Lear* can be seen in casting him as the fool, and an idea of his range is indicated by his non-comic roles: Richmond in *Richard III* (1853) and Autolycus in Wallack's *Winter's Tale* (1858). His greatest role, however, was the First Gravedigger in *Hamlet;* unlike others he never ad libbed jokes, and Walter Leman pronounced his characterization perfect. In fact, Leman adds, when Barry was demoted to Second Gravedigger, he died of a broken heart.

Comics were always favorites, though few became known as Shakespeareans. Genteel comics made people laugh with funny lines, low comedians with visual humor. Their talent was treasured in trying times, and many became stars of a particular kind: "Yankee" or "Irish" comics were familiar types, but there were others, like Joseph Jefferson with Rip Van Winkle, who created whole characters and thereby made themselves legends. For the most part, however, their reputations died with them, for humor is as evanescent as the life of its creator.

40. *Golden Era, February 7, 1858.*

## *Utility People*

Utility players were more or less character types, but they did not have a straight "line." They were cast in small roles as needed, often doubling, sometimes tripling in parts. They were of the most varied kind: young actors learning their craft, untalented players who simply loved the theater, and amateurs. All were useful to the company although they were not of first or even second quality.

They had no special line. They could, and often did, play comic parts, old age, youth, and occasionally "walking people" to fill up a crowd. They could be called upon to be an aristocrat one scene, a servant in the next. Those who remained in the utility category all their lives were probably the truest lovers of the theater, for the rewards, aside from applause, were the most meager. Since everyone in a small company worked backstage, they usually helped out as stage hands, property masters, or costumers.

Yet in spite of their usefulness, they are almost completely unknown unless they grew into the ranks of the named actors. This seems lamentable, for like all journeymen from leading players to characters, they were the essential fabric of a theater. They might not glitter, but they provided the rich background on which the jeweled stars were seen at their best.

# Conclusion

The Gold Rush was over by 1856. It ended, not with a bang, but with the gradual transformation of the West from a wilderness into the general pattern of American culture. Small rambunctious towns gradually disappeared, larger ones became respectable. Prospecting was for trained geologists; the search for gold was no longer a matter of washing nuggets from mountain streams, but of digging deep into the earth with machines. Mining had grown into big business run by big companies with offices at the big lodes. Prospectors had become working miners with regular paychecks and wives and families, with no time, no money, no *need* for Shakespeare.

By the end of the Civil War, the changes were obvious although the war itself had little direct effect on California. Sympathizers on both sides took a keen interest in the conflict and some went east to join the army, but the state as a whole was too far away for major involvement. The theater, of course, was affected, but only obliquely. Loyalty to one cause or the other, along with the dangers of travel, kept most American actors from travelling. English and Australian players, wishing to avoid the conflict, were more likely to visit California than New York, but their numbers were few. Amateur productions flourished, and most professional companies relied more on native favorites than visiting stars.

As the isolation from the Eastern mainstream continued, the West developed a slightly different style in acting, and players who moved from one coast to the other were often criticized by local standards. Eastern critics considered Western actors rough and flamboyant, Western critics regarded Eastern actors as too studied. It would take half a century before the two styles would begin to merge.

This is not to suggest no more stars came nor that Shakespearean plays were not given. After 1865, Californians saw Charlotte Cushman, Edwin Forrest and John McCullough; Edwin Booth returned with Lawrence Barrett, and a host of others followed, bringing with them their own special brand of Shakespeare. Some were fairly exotic. On March 25, 1868, San Francisco was treated to a polyglot *Othello* in which actors delivered their lines in their native tongues. Othello, played by George Pauncefort, spoke English, the rest were a mixture of French, German and Danish.[1]

Beyond the war and the concomitant isolation, other significant changes in the East would have a direct effect on theater in the rest of the country. The repertory system, which required an actor to keep between fifteen and twenty parts fresh at all times, received a rude jolt during the 1865–66 season in New York: Edwin Booth played *Hamlet* for 100 consecutive nights. This event was not only important in theatrical history but initiated a vast change in the system itself.

The repercussions began to be felt in the following season when *The Black Crook* began its phenomenal run of 475 nights. Running a single play with a single cast was so much more lucrative than repertory that other New York managers began looking for similar bonanzas. By 1868, Sol Smith was already complaining about the practice of running one play for as long as possible, thus cutting down on the opportunities for actors. His arguments went unheeded, and although repertory did not immediately disappear, by 1870 the long run was a permanently established pattern on Broadway.

Even away from New York, the end of repertory came swiftly:

1. *Theatre Research Project, 10677, Vol. 9, pp. 117–118.*

in 1871, there were fifty permanent companies, in 1878, only seven or eight, by 1899, none at all. They were replaced by a combination of limited repertory and the star system which meant essentially a stock company offering three or four plays to display a star. The stock might include Shakespeare, but more often than not, the works were either written for the star or selected with an eye to his or her special talents. Actors became identified with single plays: James O'Neill with *The Count of Monte Cristo,* William Gillette with *Sherlock Holmes,* Joseph Jefferson with *Rip Van Winkle,* and Otis Skinner with *Kismet.*

The other significant change came in 1869. The transcontinental railroad meant that Eastern managers could put together their own shows with their own stars and their own companies, what today would be called a "package." Broadway stars travelled in style with private coaches and whole boxcars of scenery and costumes. If they played Shakespeare at all, it was carefully studied, historically accurate, and elegantly mounted. Schedules planned in New York included only towns on railroad lines, and those towns, with their own well-established social strata, had definite ideas about "culture"; Shakespeare was Art for the elite.

# Bibliography

## Books

Abbott, C.S. *Recollections of a California Pioneer.* New York. Neale, 1917.

Adams, John Quincy. *Recollections of Early Theatricals in San Francisco.* An essay read before the California Historical Society, April 8, 1890.

Ashley, Mabel Celeste. "Gold Rush Theatre in Nevada City, California." Unpublished master's thesis, Stanford University, 1967.

Ayers, James J. *Gold and Sunshine.* Boston: Gorham, 1922.

Baldwin, Joseph Glover. *The Flush Times of California.* Athens: University of Georgia, 1966.

Barrett, Lawrence. *Edwin Forrest.* Boston: J.R. Osgood, 1882.

Beebe, Lucius M., and Charles M. Clegg. *Legends of the Comstock Lode.* Oakland, Calif.: Grahame Hardy, 1950.

Biggs, Donald C. *Conquer and Colonize.* San Rafael, Calif. Presidio, 1977.

Billington, Ray Allen. *Westward Expansion,* 4th ed. New York: Macmillan, 1974.

Bode, Carl. *The Anatomy of American Popular Culture, 1840–1961.* Berkeley: University of California, 1959.

Borthwick, J.D. *The Gold Hunters,* ed. Horace Kephart. New York: Doubleday, 1917.

Brackenridge, H.M. *Recollections of Persons and Places in the West.* Philadelphia: James Kay, Jr., 1834.

Branam, George C. *Eighteenth-Century Adaptations of Shakespearean Tragedy.* Berkeley: University of California, 1956.

Brown, Joel, and Ann Brown. *Gold Rush.* 2 vols. Washington (state), 1974.

Brown, T. Allston. *History of the American Stage.* New York: Dick & Fitz-gerald, 1870.

_____. *History of the New York Stage from the First Performance in 1732 to 1901.* New York: Dodd, Mead, 1903.

Buck, Franklin A. *A Yankee Trader in the Gold Rush,* ed. Katherine A. White. Boston: Houghton Mifflin, 1930.

Buckbee, Edna Bryan. *The Saga of Old Tuolumne.* New York: Press of the Pioneers, 1935.

Burnett, Peter H. *Recollections and Opinions of an Old Pioneer.* New York: Da Capo, 1969.

Carson, William G.B., ed. *Letters of Mr. and Mrs. Charles Kean.* St. Louis: Washington University, 1948.

_____. *Managers in Distress.* St. Louis: St. Louis Historical Documents Foundation, 1949.

_____. *The Theatre on the Frontier.* Chicago: Benjamin Blom, 1965.

Chamberlain, Samuel E. *My Confession.* New York: Harper, 1956.

Christman, Enos. *One Man's Gold.* New York: McGraw Hill, 1930.

Clarke, Asia Booth. *The Elder and the Younger Booth.* New York: Outing, 1882.

Coad, Oral Sumner, and Edwin Mims, Jr. *The American Stage.* New Haven: Yale, 1929.

Coffin, George A. *A Pioneer Voyage to California and Around the World, 1849–1852.* Chicago: Gorham B. Coffin, 1908.

Colton, Walter. *Three Years in California.* New York: A.S. Barnes, 1850.

Conolly, L.W. *Theatrical Touring and Founding in North America.* London: Greenwood, 1982.

Cowell, Joe. *Thirty Years Passed among the Actors and Actresses of England and America.* New York: Harper, 1844.

Cox, Isaac. *The Annals of Trinity County.* San Francisco: Commercial Book and Job Steam Printing Establishment, 1858.

Coy, Owen Cochran. *Gold Days.* Los Angeles: Powell, 1929.

Creahan, John. *The Life of Laura Keene, Actress, Artist, Manager and Scholar.* Philadelphia: Rodgers, 1897.

Davidge, William. *Footlight Flashes.* New York: American News, 1866.

Davis, H.P. *Gold Rush Days in Nevada City.* Nevada City: Berliner & McGinnis, 1948.

Davis, William A. *Seventy-Five Years in California.* San Francisco: Howell, 1929.

Delano, Alonzo. *California Correspondence,* ed. Irving McKee. Sacramento: Book Collectors Club, 1952.

DeVoto, Bernard. *Mark Twain's America.* Boston: Houghton Mifflin, 1932.

Dorman, James H., Jr. *Theater in the Ante-Bellum South, 1815–1861.* Chapel Hill: University of North Carolina. 1967.

Ducasse, George. *San Francisco Theatre Research,* ed. Lawrence Estavan. San Francisco: WPA Project 8386, vol. 3, 1939.

————, and Matthew Gateley. *San Francisco Theatre Research,* ed. Lawrence Estavan. San Francisco: WPA Project 10677, vol. 9, 1939.

Dunn, Esther C. *Shakespeare in America.* New York: Macmillan, 1939.

Early, Stepehn. *Columbia.* San Francisco: Fearon, 1957.

Engle, Gary D., ed. *This Grotesque Essence: Plays from the Minstrel Stage.* Baton Rouge: Louisiana State University, 1978.

Ford, George D. *These Were Actors.* New York: Library, 1955.

Fox, Harrison. *Edwin Forrest.* San Francisco: WPA Project 10677, vol. 11, 1940.

Gaer, Joseph. *The Theatre of the Gold Rush Decade in San Francisco.* (Monograph 5). San Francisco: California Literary Research, State Emergency Relief Administration Project, 1935.

Gagey, Edmond M. *The San Francisco Stage.* New York: Columbia, 1950.

Giffen, Guy J. *California Expedition.* Oakland: Biobooks, 1951.

Glasscock, C.B. *The Big Bonanza: The Story of the Comstock Lode.* Indianapolis: Bobbs-Merrill, 1931.

Grant, Howard F. *The Story of Seattle's Early Theatres.* Seattle: University of Washington, 1934.

Grimsted, David. *Melodrama Unveiled: American Theater and Culture, 1800-1850.* Chicago: University of Chicago Press, 1968.

Hackett, James H. *Notes and Comments upon Certain Plays and Actors of Shakespeare, with Criticisms and Correspondence.* New York: Carleton, 1864.

Harrison, Alan. *Junius Brutus Booth et al.* San Francisco: WPA Project 8386, vol. 4, 1938

————, and Eddie Shimano. *John McCullough.* San Francisco: WPA Project 8386, vol. 6, 1936.

Henderson, Myrtle E. *A History of the Theatre in Salt Lake City.* Evanston, Ill.: The Author, 1936.

Hillyer, Katherine, and Katherine Best. *The Amazing Story of Piper's Opera House.* Virginia City, Nevada: Enterprise Press, 1953.

Hoole, Stanley. *The Ante-Bellum Charleston Theatre.* Tuscaloosa: University of Alabama, 1946.

Hornblow, Arthur. *History of the Theatre in America from Its Beginning to the Present Time.* 2 vols. Philadelphia: Lippincott, 1919.

Hutton, Laurence. *Curiosities of the American Stage.* New York: Harper, 1931.

Jackson, Alfred T. *Diary of a Forty-Niner,* ed. Chauncy L. Canfield. San Francisco: Shepard, 1906.

Jackson, Joseph Henry. *Anybody's Gold: The Story of California's Mining Towns.* New York: Appleton-Century, 1941.

Jacobson, Pauline. *City of the Golden Fifties.* Berkeley: University of California, 1941.

Jennings, John S. *Theatrical and Social Life; or Secrets of the Stage: Greenroom and Sawdust Areas.* St. Louis: Herbert & Cole, 1886.

Kendall, John S. *The Golden Age of the New Orleans Theater.* Baton Rouge: Louisiana State University, 1952.

Kimmel, Stanley. *The Mad Booths of Maryland.* New York: Bobbs-Merrill, 1940.

Lambourne, Alfred A. *A Playhouse.* Salt Lake City: Harwood & Richards, n.d.

Leavitt, M.B. *Fifty Years of Theatrical Management.* New York: Broadway, 1912.

Leman, Walter M. *Memoirs of an Old Actor.* San Francisco: Roman, 1886.

Lengyel, Cornel, and Eddie Shimano. *San Francisco Theatre Research,* ed. Lawrence Estavan. San Francisco: WPA Project 8386, vol. 2, 1938.

Leverton, Garrett H. *The Production of Late Nineteenth-Century Drama.* New York: Columbia University, 1936.

Lindsay, John Shanks. *The Mormons and the Theatre.* Salt Lake City: Century, 1905.

Ludlow, Noah Miller. *Dramatic Life as I Found It.* St. Louis: G.I. Jones, 1880.

McCabe, John J. "Journal." Unpublished manuscript in California State Library.

Macgowan, Kenneth. *Footlights Across America.* New York: Harcourt, Brace, 1929.

MacMinn, George R. *The Theater of the Golden Era in California.* Caldwell, Idaho: Caxton, 1941.

Marder, Louis. *His Exits and His Entrances: The Story of Shakespeare's Reputation.* New York: Lippincott, 1963.

Margetts, Ralph Elliott. "A Study of the Theatrical Career of Julia Dean Hayne." Unpublished doctoral disseration, University of Utah, 1959.

Matthews, Brander, and Lawrence Hutton, eds. *Actors and Actresses of Great Britain and the United States.* 2 vols. New York: Cassell, 1886.

Maughan, Ila Fisher. *Pioneer Theatre in the Desert.* Salt Lake City: Deseret, 1961.

Mighels, Ella Sterling. *Literary California: Poetry and Portraits.* San Francisco: Harr Wagner, 1918.

Miller, William C. "An Historical Study of the Theatrical Entertainment in Virginia City, Nevada." Unpublished doctoral dissertation, University of Southern California, 1947.

Moody, Richard. *Edwin Forrest: First Star of the American Stage.* New York: Knopf, 1960.

Morris, Lloyd. *Curtain Time: The Story of the American Theater.* New York: Random House, 1953.

Moses, Montrose, and John Mason Brown, eds. *The American Theatre as Seen by Its Critics, 1752-1934.* New York: W.W. Norton, 1934.

_____. *The Fabulous Forrest.* Boston: Little, Brown, 1929.

_____. *Famous Actor-Families in America.* New York: Crowell, 1906.

Murdoch, James E. *The Stage; or, Recollections of Actors and Acting from an Experience of Fifty Years.* Philadelphia: J.M. Stoddart, 1880.

Neville, Amelia Ransome. *The Fantastic City: Memoirs of the Social and Romantic Life of Old San Francisco.* New York: Houghton Mifflin, 1932.

Page, L.C. *Famous Actresses.* Boston: Page, 1902.

_____. *Famous Players.* Boston: Page, 1903.

Paul, Rodman. *California Gold: The Beginnings of Mining in the Far West.* Cambridge, Mass.: Harvard University Press, 1947.

Perkins, William. *Journal,* ed. Dale L. Morgan and James R. Scobie. Los Angeles: UCLA, 1964.

Phelps, H.P. *Players of a Century.* Albany, N.Y.: Joseph McDonough, 1880.

Pond, James Burton. *Eccentricities of Genius.* New York: G.W. Killingham, 1900.

Pyper, George D. *The Romance of an Old Playhouse.* Salt Lake City: Seagull, 1937.

Rather, Lois. *Bonanza Theater.* Oakland: Rather, 1977.

Rourke, Constance. *Troupers of the Gold Coast; or, the Rise of Lotta Crabtree.* New York: Harcourt, Brace, 1928.

Ruggles, Eleanor. *Prince of Players.* New York. W.W. Norton, 1953.

Rusk, Ralph Leslie. *The Literature of the Middle Western Frontier.* New York: Columbia, 1925.

Scherer, James A.B. *The First Forty-Niner.* New York: Minton Balch, 1925.

Schoberlin, Melvin. *From Candles to Footlights.* Denver: Old West, 1941.

Seilhamer, G O *An Interviewer's Album.* New York: Alvin Perry, 1881.

Shattuck, Charles H. *The Hamlet of Edwin Booth.* Urbana: University of Illinois, 1969.

_____. *Shakespeare on the American Stage: From the Hallams to Edwin Booth.* Washington, D.C.: Folger Shakespeare Library, 1976.

Simon, Henry W. *The Reading of Shakespeare in American Schools and Colleges: An Historical Survey.* New York: Simon and Schuster, 1932.

Sinnott, James J. *Downieville: Gold Town on the Yuba.* Volcano: California Traveller, 1972.

Smith, Sol. *Theatrical Apprenticeship and Anecdotal Reflections of Sol Smith.* Philadelphia: Carey & Hart, 1846.

_____. *The Theatrical Journey.* Philadelphia: T.B. Peterson, 1854.

_____. *Theatrical Management in the West and South for Thirty Years.* New York: Harper, 1868.

Soule, Frank, John H. Gihon, and Hames Nisbet. *The Annals of San Francisco.* Palo Alto: Lewis Osborne, 1866.

Sprague, Arthur Colby. *Shakespearean Players and Performances.* Cambridge, Mass: Harvard University Press, 1953.

Stewart, George R. "The Drama in a Frontier Theater," *Essays in Dramatic Literature.* Princeton: Princeton University Press, 1935.

Stoddart, James H. *Recollections of a Player.* New York: Century, 1902.

Stone, Henry D. *Personal Recollections of the Drama.* Albany, N.Y.: Charles Van Benthuysen, 1873.

Strang, Lewis. *Players and Plays of the Last Quarter Century,* 2 vols. Boston: L.C. Page, 1893.

Taylor, Justus H [Harlan Page Halsey]. *Joe Taylor, Barnstormer.* New York: Jenkins, 1913.

Victor, Frances Fuller. *The River of the West.* Hartford, 1871.

Warde, Frederick. *Fifty Years of Make-Believe.* New York: International, 1920.

Watson, Douglas. *California in the Fifties.* San Francisco: John Howell, 1936.

Watson, Margaret G. *Silver Theatre: Amusements of Nevada's Mining Frontier, 1850–1854.* Glendale, Calif.: Arthur H. Clark, 1964.

Webb, Nancy, and Jean Francis. *Will Shakespeare and His America.* New York: Viking, 1964.

Wells, Stanley, ed. *Nineteenth-Century Shakespeare Burlesques.* 5 vols. Wilmington, Del.: Michael Glazier, 1978.

Whitney, H.G. *The Drama of Utah: The Story of the Salt Lake Theatre.* Salt Lake City: Deseret News, 1915.

Willson, Clair Eugene. *Mimes and Miners.* Tucson: University of Arizona Bulletin, 6, 7 (October, 1935).

Wilson, Garff B. *A History of American Acting.* Bloomington: Indiana University, 1966.

————. *Three Hundred Years of American Drama and Theatre.* Englewood Cliffs, N.J.: Prentice-Hall, 1973.

Winter, William. *Shakespeare on the Stage.* New York: Moffat, Yard, 1916.

Wyman, Walker D., ed. *California Emigrant Letters.* New York: Bookman, 1952.

## *Articles*

"The American Theater," *The Palimpsest* **31,** 1 (January, 1950), 8–23.

Booth, Edwin. "Some Words about My Father, " in *Kean and Booth and Their Contemporaries,* ed. Brander Matthews and L. Hutton. Boston: L. Page, 1900.

Browne, Ray B. "Shakespeare in America: Vaudeville and Negro Minstrelsy," *American Quarterly* **12,** 3 (Fall, 1960), 374–391.

Davidson, Levett J. "Shakespeare in the Rockies," *Shakespeare Quarterly* **4** (January, 1953), 39–49.

Davis, Mrs. Sam P. "Early Theatrical Attractions in Carson," *Nevada State Historical Society Papers, 1923-1924*, pp. 201-212.

Denny, Reuel. "The Discovery of Popular Culture," in *American Perspectives: The National Self-Image in the Twentieth Century*, ed. Robert E. Spiller and Eric Larrabee. Cambridge, Mass.: Harvard University Press, 1961.

Evans, Joseph. "Around Cape Horn with Colonel Stevenson's Regiment in 1846," *Society of California Pioneers Quarterly* **7**, 4 (December, 1930), 244-254.

Falk, Robert. "Shakespeare in America: A Survey to 1900," *Shakespeare Survey* **18** (1965), 102-118.

Gates, William Bryan. "Performances of Shakespeare in Ante-Bellum Mississippi," *Journal of Mississippi History* **5**, 1 (January, 1943), 28-37.

Lawrence, J.E. "The Drama in the Pacific: First Theatricals in California," *Golden Era*, April 7, 15, and 20, May 13, 1855.

Levine, Lawrence W. "William Shakespeare and the American People: A Study in Cultural Transformation," *American Historical Review* **89** (February, 1984), 34-66.

McManaway, James G. "Shakespeare in the United States," *PMLA* **79** (December, 1964), 513-518.

Moffatt, Walter. "First Theatrical Activities in America," *Arkansas Historical Quarterly* **12** (Winter, 1953), 327-332.

Perrigo, Lynn. "The First Two Decades of Central City Theatricals," *Colorado Magazine* **11**, 4 (July, 1934), 141-152.

Reeves, Robert N. "Abraham Lincoln's Knowledge of Shakespeare," *Overland Monthly* **43** (Easter, 1904), 336-342.

Rodecape, Lois Foster [Rather]. "Tom Maguire, Napoleon of the Stage," *California Historical Society Quarterly* **20**, 4 (December, 1941), 289-314; **21**, 1 (March, 1942), 39-74; **21**, 2 (June, 1942), 141-182; **21**, 3 (September, 1942), 239-275.

Roppolo, Joseph Patrick. "Hamlet in New Orleans," *Tulane Studies in English* **6** (1956), 71-85.

Sayre, Hal. "Early Central City Theatricals and Other Reminiscences," *The Colorado Magazine* **6**, 2 (March, 1929), 47-52.

Stewart, Georg R., Jr. "The Drama in a Frontier Theatre," pp. 183-204 in *Essays in Dramatic Literature*, ed. Hardin Craig. Princeton: Princeton University Press, 1935.

Thorndike, Ashley. "Shakespeare in America," in *Aspects of Shakespeare, Being British Academy Lectures*, ed. L. Abercrombie. Oxford: Clarendon, 1933.

Van Orman, Richard A. "The Bard in the West," *Western Historical Quarterly* **5** (January, 1974), 29-38.

Williams, Gary Jay. "Madam Vestris' *A Midsummer Night's Dream* and the Web of Victorian Tradition," *Theatre Survey*, **18**, 2 (November, 1977), 1-22.

## Newspapers

*Alta California,* 1849–1860
*Amador Sentinel,* 1854
*California Express,* 1851–1866
*California Spirit of the Times and Fireman's Journal,* 1852–1865
*Columbia Gazette,* 1851–1853
*Dutch Flat Enquirer,* 1862–1865
*Era,* 1881
*Golden Era,* 1863–1868
*Grass Valley National,* 1863–1865
*Humboldt Times,* 1856–1857, 1863–1865
*Marysville Appeal Democrat,* 1861–1865
*Marysville Daily Evening Herald,* 1851–1854, 1857–1865
*Mountain Echo,* 1852–1853
*Mountain Messenger,* 1864
*Nevada City Nugget,* 1851–1857
*Nevada City Transcript,* 1860–1865
*New York Clipper,* 1853–1860
*New York Dramatic Mirror,* 1903
*Oroville Weekly Butte,* 1853–1857
*The Pioneer; or California Monthly Magazine,* 1854–1855
*Placer Times,* 1856–1857
*Red Bluff Beacon,* 1861–1865
*Reese River Reveille,* 1863
*Sacramento Daily Union,* 1856–1858
*Sacramento Placer Times,* 1849–1851
*San Francisco Bulletin,* 1859–1860
*San Francisco Daily Globe,* 1856–1858
*San Francisco Daily Morning Call,* 1856–1860
*San Francisco Daily National,* 1858–1860
*San Francisco Daily Whig and Commercial Advertiser,* 1852–1854
*San Francisco Evening Journal,* 1852–1856
*San Francisco Evening Picayune,* 1850–1853
*San Francisco Times,* 1857–1865
*San Francisco Herald,* 1861
*Shasta Republican,* 1855–1857
*Sonora Herald,* 1854–1864
*Stockton Daily Argus,* 1857–1865
*Trinity Journal,* 1856, 1861

# Index